Never Say "NO COMMENT"

Ian Taylor & George Olds

How
Spin
Doctors
Answer
Questions

Published in Canada
by
LB Publishing Services · Toronto · Canada

**National Library of Canada
Cataloguing in Publication Data**

Taylor, Ian, 1950-
    **Never say "no comment" : how spin doctors answer questions /
Ian Taylor and George Olds.**

ISBN   0-9697369-3-2

    1. Public relations.   2. Public relations—Language.   I. Olds,
George, 1951-   II. Title.

HM1221.T39 2003   659.2   C2003-900657-3

C O N T E N T S:

Chapter 1: Good Spin Doctors Never Say "No comment." 1

Chapter 2: The One Minute Power Message — Part One 17
Managing the Message:
      Constructing it
      Organizing it
      Writing it

Chapter 3: The One Minute Power Message — Part Two 27
Managing the Message:
      Delivering it
      Remembering it
      Sticking to it — no matter what you're asked

Chapter 4: Headline News 35

Chapter 5: Welcome To 2012 And A Place Called Big City 39
Looking at Big City Transit
Seeing the challenges facing transit services
Introducing our first student

Chapter 6: Tom Meets The Reporter From Hell 45
Ambush questions
Failure to negotiate
Saying "No comment"

Chapter 7: Tom Learns Some Basics **47**
Positioning yourself as:
       Public-spirited
       Plain-talking
       Professional
Tips on:
       Core words
       Common sense language
       Speaking like TEACHERS
Customer Service Communications Model:
       Making yourself aware
       Showing you care
       Doing your share

Chapter 8: Headline News **68**

Chapter 9: Tom Learns What "No Comment" Can Do **71**
Three major mistakes in a media encounter:
       Failing to understand the control relationship
       Falling for negative and trap questions
       Failing to structure and format your answers
Spin Defined

Chapter 10: Tom Makes Some Notes On Where He Went Wrong **79**

Chapter 11: The Spin Doctor's Game **81**
Predicting negative words in horror questions
Re-defining the issue with YOUR words
The 3-it
Tips on avoiding:
       Reactive statements
       Defensive statements
       Negative statements

Chapter 12: Tanya's Interview **95**
An expert takes control as:
       Public-spirited
       Plain-talking
       Professional

Chapter 13: SPIN College Tools. **101**
Control support techniques:
      Going directly to message
      Remind, repeat, renegotiate
      Style, enthusiasm, emotion, concern
Support statements and phrases:
      Bridges, baits and re-asks
      Techniques to handle questions
      Delivering your message
Plus:
      Power Pillars
      Building on the simple 3-it structure
      Answering and not answering the question

Chapter 14: Headline News. **120**

Chapter 15: Controversy: Which Side Are You On? **123**
Finding common ground:
      Controversial words
      Extreme words
      Common sense words
Plus:
      Looking at triangles

Chapter 16: Big City Takes A Survey. **135**
Tom handles questions involving:
      Speculation
      Personal opinions
      Reacting to others
It all comes together:
      He builds solid media relations
      He smiles on live TV
      He goes for results

Chapter 17: Headline News. **145**

Chapter 18: Tanya's Promotion **147**
The real issues here are:
>Improved customer service
>Better safety for our workers
>Savings for the customer

Chapter 19: Of Course There's A Third Student **163**
Issues of:
>Safety
>Economy
>Privacy

Appendix. **169**
Playing The Spin Doctor's Game: It's Your Turn
Opportunity Words from the Reporter From Hell
Extra copies of **One Minute Power Message** template
Biographies of the authors
Other books, courses and keynotes offered by the authors

Chapter 1

Good Spin Doctors Never Say "No comment."

What is this book about?

This book is about answering tough questions using the skills of professional spokespersons.

It's about the work of those special word-crafters, (some call them spin doctors) who find that better word, that better phrase, that better way of saying things, regardless of the audience.

Even if you never speak to the news media, this book will make you a better communicator.

We've based it on our "**Managing Your Message**" courses, where we challenge students three ways: *Do you have a message? Do you believe it? Can you say it like you mean it?* Then we give them the skills to succeed in defining, developing and delivering that message.

Who's the target audience for this book?

This book is for anyone who communicates — with the public, with customers, or with co-workers, friends and family.

It was written for people who may represent their organization publicly, and whose job involves answering questions from the media. Or from issues groups. Or customers, bosses, or co-workers.

It was written for people who may be asked questions in meetings — at the boardroom table, or at the dining room table.

It was written for anyone whose job, project or cause may require them to answer questions.

Questions about what you're doing, who you're doing it for, why you're doing it and how you're doing it.

This book shows that it's not the questions that can get you into trouble — it's the answers.

We'll ▶ help you avoid some of the most common traps in answering questions.

▶ teach you to replace the words in a question with the words in your answer.

▶ show you how to structure your message and deliver it with ease.

Our clients are mostly public organizations who are required to have something to say to the news media regularly. They're in the news every day.

They're often agencies with official spokespersons for various departments or levels within the organization who speak to various publics.

We serve people from frontline government agencies, to police departments, hospitals, transit services, the justice system, the travel industry, non-profit community groups, and even corporations.

Whenever our clients have something to say, it reflects on their **reputation**, especially when a crisis or emergency occurs and the issues hit the front pages of the newspapers and the six o'clock news.

Definition — Reputation and Issues Management

Reputation and issues management is the practice of managing various messages, by word and/or deed, in order to influence public perception and opinion.

It's about making sure you're seen by the right people to be doing the right thing, at the right time, for the right reasons.

What's a good spin doctor?

Aren't they all liars or con artists?

Good spin doctors are people who are good word-crafters. Some writers and public relations people don't like the words *spin doctor*. The media and the public often perceive the term negatively. That usually happens when the spinning is done poorly and the message is unbelievable and obviously untrue.

Spin doctors have been around as long as there's been communication and efforts to improve communication. Princes, potentates and popes have either been spin doctors or have hired them — as speechwriters, authors, editors, scribes, advisors, consultants, journalists or publicists.

Some PR and communications people vehemently deny they're spin doctors. In fact, the more some folks deny it, the more convinced the public becomes that they **are** spin doctors.

Saying "We're not spin doctors" is like saying, "The President is **not** a MORON!"

Good spin doctors don't deny; they choose to use different words — better words to communicate their messages.

How does the public perceive "No comment"?

Saying "No comment" is rude. It sounds like you're uninformed about the issue, or that you don't care enough about people to answer their questions, even if it's a reporter doing the asking. And it sure sounds like you aren't doing anything about the issue either.

Besides, it's a wasted answer. It's certainly not the best answer, especially when you do have something better to say.

When you say it to answer a reporter's question, you're saying it to the *publics* that the reporter will reach.

The final recipients of that little message will interpret your "No comment" according to their own knowledge and position on the topic of the question.

They'll hear the words filtered through their own biases, prejudices and experiences at that particular moment.

Saying "No comment" implies *you're unaware, don't care and failing to do your share* to deal with the issue at hand.

Why does it seem that the news media trap people into saying "No comment"?

We read or hear the phrase every day, most often in response to a negative question. "Are you responsible for that disaster (*train derailment, oil spill, bureaucratic boondoggle* — take your pick)?"

A "No comment" answer draws attention to the question. It can sound like you **are** responsible, like you are hiding facts, or withholding information. It sounds like you're afraid to answer the question for fear it will incriminate you.

The public perception is that you've done something wrong, otherwise why would you be hiding or withholding information.

Saying "No comment" is like saying "We're guilty." Those two words say a lot about you (or your organization).

You've created a controversial answer right when you'd probably prefer to avoid controversy.

Most good reporters work to balance their news stories, so if one side of the story says "No comment," the other side gets to tell their story more completely. The other side of the issue gets all the coverage, while the "No comment" side is seen to be hiding. This can create controversy or conflict where it may not have existed before.

> ▷ **Tip:** Not returning a reporter's call is considered the same as saying "No comment" in most newsrooms.

Won't a "No comment" answer keep you out of trouble?

Nope. It's often perceived as a negative, defensive and reactive message, delivered under pressure right when there's public concern, interest or a need for more information.

Would you say "No comment" to an upset, angry or enquiring customer? Would you keep the customer if you did? What would that customer tell others?

▶ It's *negative* because it contains the word no. Instead, you might want to indicate you'll have something to say later.

▶ It's *defensive* because it misses an opportunity to state your message, even if your message consists of saying you're anxious to learn more before answering.

▶ It's *reactive* because it ties the answer directly to the question, no matter what the question was. The spin all takes place around the negative word or words in the question.

If you think "No comment" will keep you out of trouble, wait until you meet our students later in this book. They'll face tough issues — in the year 2012.

So, when you say "No comment" you're in fact, making a comment?

Yes, it can have the same effect as a comment.

For instance, let's say there have been some problems in your organization's budget. The question is, "What do you think of the latest screw-up in your organization today? Is someone playing fast and loose with the numbers here?"

If you answer "No comment," it sounds like there are probably some major money problems going on; that you might just be a big part of those problems.

What if the next question is, "Do you accept responsibility for this situation?"

What would saying "No comment" imply now?

A "No comment" answer may give the impression you really are in trouble. Or you might suddenly have created trouble when none existed before.

Maybe your best message is to say you're "anxious to find out what's happening, so that we can work on it as soon as possible."

Maybe it's better for someone else to answer the question. If so, **refer** the questioner to the right source.

Maybe you don't know the answer. Say so, and then offer to get the information later. Here you are **deferring** the question. You're buying time for strategic purposes — to give you time to get the information that will help you define, develop and deliver your answer.

It's better to stick to a carefully prepared message rather than become reactive, say the wrong thing, or to say the first thing that pops into your head, before you've had time to think.

Is "No comment" what you intended to say? The best you have to say?

We happen to believe that if you have nothing to say about a certain issue, you should say nothing.

It is sometimes far better to keep your mouth shut than to say "No comment" and show you're rude, uninformed or guilty.

We see people refusing to comment all the time, right? Especially lawyers, police and bureaucrats.

You won't see our students doing that, and we train lots of lawyers, police and bureaucrats. You can see our students almost any day in the Toronto and Canadian news media and they're not saying "No comment."

Each of those students has gone through some rigorous training to convince them to **go to message** and **stay on message**.

We find that each of them has a distinct personality and a distinct way of analyzing every question. Some get all hung up on the exactness of the wording and they become *literalistic analyzers*. For the literalist, the problem is in that word *comment*. If they're asked for a comment, they're inclined to offer a comment, even if it gets them into trouble.

Very few of us are in the business of commenting on an issue, unless we're providing a personal opinion as a citizen or taxpayer or person on the street.

Commenting is the job of commentators or politicians or editorialists — sometimes called pundits.

Media pundits comment on an issue, because they're seen as outside experts. Commentators often get paid for their quickness with a quip, their on-camera experience and their name recognition. They talk in *sound-bites,* they're interesting and they've got experience.

You likely get paid to represent your organization's position without a commentary. Your job is likely to involve **informing**, **describing and explaining**, not commenting.

Editorialists, reporters and media columnists can provide a commentary or viewpoint or opinion simply with their choice of words to describe a situation. It's called media spin.

What's media spin?

Here's a typical media spin situation:

> The city's transit company announces a 10 percent fare increase. There is naturally lots of opposition to it from many individuals and groups who have an interest in the issue.
>
> There are two different newspapers in the city, each with it's own political slant or position. Each newspaper will decide if the matter is news, how that news will be presented and what approach, angle or slant will be taken in its delivery, starting with the headline.
>
> Here are two very different headlines that might result from the same announcement about an increase in transit fares:

Riders gouged in fare boost, Mayor says

Or...

Fare increase to fund faster fleet, Transit says

In these two different headlines we see an example of different media spin being applied to the same basic news story. If you like and support the Mayor, you'll like and support the spin in the first headline.

In the first case, an opportunistic politician has created negative headlines for political purposes and the newspaper has applied a certain negative spin. In the second case, the transit company has succeeded in getting a more positive spin on the story.

Why the differences in the media's spin?

In the first case, the Mayor's negative message, for whatever reason, was able to influence the headline. Maybe the media outlet supports the Mayor or the Mayor's position on this issue.

In the second headline, the transit company succeeded in influencing the choice of words and the angle of the story. Maybe the transit company is a large advertiser. Maybe the newspaper doesn't support the Mayor. Sometimes you win, sometimes you don't.

There are all kinds of things that could happen to influence the choice to go with this headline, this angle, this spin.

- Maybe the negative headline would sell more newspapers.
- Maybe the news outlet has its own agenda or political purpose.
- Maybe the real spin lies somewhere between these two headlines.

There's an old saying: "There's always three sides to a story: your version, my version and the truth." These different headlines are simply different words chosen to define the different versions of the story. And that's all spin is, really — your version of the story. The recipients of the story get to decide what is the truth.

So are you suggesting that spin is the media's fault?

Spin is largely about word choice and delivery.

▶ Anyone who writes is practising spin.

▶ Anyone who re-writes or edits a document is practising spin. They feel they've chosen a better word than the original — a better way of saying something.

▶ Anyone who chooses words to speak, write or communicate is exercising a form of spin.

If you choose words that are so positive that nobody believes them, you've failed at being a spin doctor. But if you can find the best words to describe and define a situation, and most people agree on your definition, you've succeeded in your spin.

If you say that you really care, but can't show or prove that you care, you've failed at spin. Why would the media or anyone believe you if you can't prove it? If you can explain three actions you're taking because you care, you'll succeed at spin.

When a headline is written, the media's spin is applied.

Media spin is applied when a decision is made to put a news story on page one or page none.

Media spin is applied when editors choose what photograph to run of a politician. Is she shown on the front page dropping a football during a private moment, or is she shown handing out a cheque to help a community group in a staged, boring event? Which photo would you pick if you were the photo editor? Wouldn't you be exercising spin?

Saying "No comment" is simply bad spin. You can avoid commenting without speaking those words.

OK, let's get this straight. We should not be commenting, yet at the same time we should avoid that particular little phrase, "No comment." Is that about it?

Pretty much.

Most professional spokespersons will not be paid to express personal opinions or to make a comment on behalf of their organization, no matter how fantastic their opinions or comment may be.

As a spokesperson, you're paid to speak on behalf of your organization or corporation, not for yourself, just as reporters are required to serve the interests of whoever pays their salary.

Reporters who ask you to comment are choosing words that are part of their lexicon, not yours.

When you're asked to comment, don't take it literally. Interpret most questions as an invitation to speak about whatever it is you're there to speak about. Speak about what you agreed to speak about and stick to it. Go directly to your planned message, once you have one.

Your job is often to brief a reporter — to inform, explain or describe — not to face an inquisition.

A good, solid **media briefing** should contain messages that will deal with the toughest questions that may arise. That way, you'll be able to answer the questions, to **refer** them elsewhere or to **defer** them until more information is available.

This book will teach you some techniques to become a better writer, thinker and speaker, in the style of a professional media spokesperson or spin doctor.

We get to work with lots of professional and amateur spokespersons. It's often a joy.

We tend to train folks who are sometimes referred to simply as, "A **spokesperson for** the police (the hospital, the city, the state or province, the government, the airline…) said today that the incident occurred shortly after noon about six kilometres north of Westhaven Mall."

Why no name? They've succeeded in providing just the essential facts, without the need for an attribution by name.

The professional spokesperson's job is to answer tough questions and avoid controversy.

The good ones seldom say "No comment."

There are exceptions to every rule, including this one.

The professionals usually say "No comment" only as a purposeful and indirect way of commenting or drawing attention to an issue. In other words, they want to use negative wording in order to be controversial.

When is it OK to say "No comment"?

Here are three examples of when you might choose to say "No comment."

1. **If you're asked if you think the Mayor has a drinking problem, and you wish to draw attention to the allegations, you could answer "No comment".**

   The answer draws attention to the Mayor's drinking problem, just when she probably hopes people would stop talking about it. You would, in effect, be commenting on the Mayor's drinking problems and keeping the issue in the news.

   You might even phrase your answer more indirectly and more negatively; perhaps saying, "It's really not appropriate for me to be commenting on the Mayor's drinking problems/marital problems/financial difficulties/nervous breakdown at this time."

   Or: "There's been a lot of folks talking about the Mayor's drinking problems, but I would never stoop so low as to get into that kind of discussion. I don't think personal problems are an issue here and I won't comment on those troubling allegations."

   You've still used the word "comment" in your answer and yet you've drawn attention to all the negative aspects of the issue. Presumably you've done it on purpose.

2. **If you are asked if there is a cover-up and you want everyone to think that there is a cover-up, say "No comment." Or say, "There's no cover-up."**

   It would be better to say, "We're putting some information together right now so we can speak to you later." Or say, "The privacy act prevents me from providing that information."

   In this case, you are deferring the question until you have more information, so what you're saying is, in effect, "We've got no information at this time but stay tuned for an update as soon as details become available."

Here's how you might refer the question elsewhere:

"You should really contact our communications office who can discuss our privacy policies."

3. **If you're asked if you're guilty and you want everyone to think you're guilty, then saying "No comment" makes you sound guilty.**

In our classes, we'll sometimes ask students if they accept personal responsibility for a particular situation or recent disaster. Saying "No comment" is an admission of guilt.

▶ When you say "No comment," you've made the question more important than the answer.

▶ When you say "No comment," you emphasize the inflammatory language in the question.

▶ When you say "No comment," you miss an opportunity to go to message.

▶ Saying "No comment" is the same as going off-message.

Haven't you broken this rule when you came up with the title of this book or used the term spin doctor?

Yes, because there are exceptions to every rule, like: Never say never.

Our company is called Never Say "NO COMMENT" Inc.

That's the name of a training course we offer, and the title of a keynote speech by Ian Taylor.

Our website: **neversaynocomment.com**

It's used as a *cliché, slogan or catchy figure of speech* so you won't forget us.

Anyone who's ever come in contact with our training is unlikely to use the term "No comment" again because we focus so much on the traps of negative messaging.

Really, would you be reading this book if it had a title like:

Some Advice Regarding Responding To Inquiries

You see, when you decide what to title a book, or an essay, or a report — you're exercising spin.

Where does message management start?

Good messaging starts by writing to an outline, anticipating questions that may come up, then formulating and expanding upon the answers. Your core messages or core statements answer core questions about your issue(s). That's why we'll make **you** the issue first.

We're going to have you start with a simple writing exercise, an introduction of yourself — your **One Minute Power Message**. You can keep it in your desk drawer or on file, to update as needed for the rest of your life. It's a message about an important issue in your life — it's about you.

You mean there's homework?

Of course, but it's a short exercise with a writing template to make it easy. It's designed to teach a lot about crafting strong core messages with a simple 3 part formula.

It's probably the easiest communications formula ever developed, and we take no credit for it.

It's been used for centuries in oral and written communication, and it's great for use in the media. It's a cornerstone method for writing speeches, briefings, marketing messages, advertising and news copy as well as television production.

We've adapted that three 3 structure to create the framework in which to define, develop and deliver your answers. The answering style we teach is easy to learn, use and remember. **We call it the 3-it**.

A 3-it can look like this:

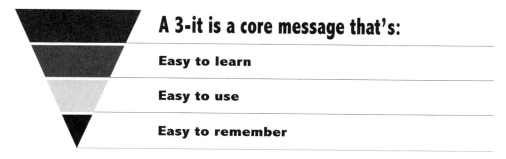

A 3-it is a core message that's:

Easy to learn

Easy to use

Easy to remember

You'll learn to expand your **One Minute Power Message** to seven minutes, simply by adding to the basic 3-it structure. Once you've learned to prepare your message, we'll show you how to go easily to that message, no matter what you're asked.

Then, we'll show you how you can start improving the way *you write, speak and think today,* by looking to the future. We'll imagine how issues might look for potential students of ours *a decade from now.* Some of their issues are already with us today.

Journalism is about the actual events of today. History is the story of those events seen from the perspective of time. Hope is about the promise of events of tomorrow. Our hope is that you'll learn a few spokespersons' techniques here, so that you won't become history.

We'll look at how three futuristic spokespersons learn their basic skills in handling tough questions about issues like transportation, utilities, privacy, safety, corporate responsibility, good government, public consultation and public services. We'll watch them become spin doctors.

Our spokespersons of the future will handle horror questions, and you'll see how they deliver answers that help them *stay on message,* without ever having to say "No comment."

Once they learn how to take control of the communications encounter, you'll see how they handle the most common form of trap — **the negative question**.

Our goals here are to teach you the skills to:

▶ control (or at least understand) the roles in a communications encounter,

▶ manage and avoid various trap or negative questions, and

▶ structure your responses for various communications formats.

Understanding control, avoiding traps, and solid structure — pretty good lessons for life, no?

So we're going to begin with **your** message about **you**.

In the next section, we give you a short form to fill out. Simply follow along, answer some easy questions and fill in the blanks.

You'll learn how to build a simple core message structure.

Then you'll learn to use your core messages to answer some tough questions.

We'll have you taking control of the encounter, handling negative questions and providing structured answers like a pro.

Enjoy and learn.

Chapter 2

The One Minute Power Message — Part 1

Managing the Message:

Constructing it

Organizing it

Writing it

It's time to get to work.

Your first task is to prepare a short introduction about yourself with a basic 3-it formula. It's called the **One Minute Power Message**.

Your name

Who: ▶ Your name, title, department, company/organization
▶ Your background, professional and personal
▶ Something unique about you, such as a hobby or noteworthy accomplishment

What: ▶ Your past, present or future work (What do you do – your job, task, responsibility)
▶ What your team (department, company/organization) does
▶ What your audience may be asked to do
(Include 3 numbers or statistics)

Why: ▶ Why your topic or message is important
▶ Why you are here
▶ Why the audience should care

A closing slogan or summary statement

INSTRUCTIONS:

Give yourself about ten minutes to write your **Power Message**. Use a stopwatch or other means to limit your time.

Why a short time limit?

You're writing to a very tight deadline because that's what happens to reporters, spokespersons and lots of us every day.

Often in our day-to-day work we're called upon to provide updates, briefings or reports without a lot of notice, so we need to learn ways to fast track our messaging.

You'll have the rest of your life to edit or add to the material after the initial draft and you'll learn to adapt this simple template for a host of core messages about issues you may face.

1. Write no more than 150 words.

W h y ?

Most people speak at about 150 words per minute.

This is a **one minute introduction**, which will presumably be read aloud by someone else, word for word, unchanged.

Why should one provide a prepared introduction?

For professional speakers, the introduction is part of the formal presentation. It is often part of their contract.

The introduction is designed to set up the audience for what you're about to say. It should present you as someone who, at this moment, with this audience, is *important, interesting and informative*.

You should not leave it up to the chair or host to ad-lib your introduction. It could be a disaster. Your introduction is an official part of your presentation.

At home, you can read the introduction out loud and time it or have someone time it for you.

Record it and play it back several times. Edit the content as required.

What about the voice?

Your personal, at-home training program should include a tape recorder so that you get used to the sound of your own voice.

The first step in improving the sound of your voice is to assess it by listening to it on tape. Then you can decide if you need to slow down or speak more quickly. Only by listening can you know when to change the pacing or adjust your pitch, breathing or volume. Listen for the syllables and consonants in each word you speak.

In our training workshops, we time your presentation, give you some feedback on your delivery and then ask the other students to report what quotable quotes or sound-bites they picked up from your introduction.

This is a listening exercise designed to show you what parts of a one-minute presentation people will recall.

Most people tend to recall *statistics, achievements and literary devices such as a slogans, metaphors, analogies, mottos, figures of speech or clichés.*

2. Write for the intended public or audience.

Prepare a unique introduction, with information specific to a particular audience at a particular time. Its purpose is *to set you up, to set the audience up, and to set the message up.*

The audience might be a high school class, a group of residents from a neighbourhood or a roomful of frontline employees. Assume the typical audience has a grade 6 to 8 comprehension level, no matter how smart they think they are.

This writing exercise provides a generic structure that you can modify for each occasion. The design, style and construction of the message will stay the same.

You should write (and speak) in a way that shows you care about your audience. We call it **common sense language**. If you can say something plainly enough, use lots of examples, and base your position on an inarguable premise, people will think that what you're saying *just makes common sense*. You'll learn more of the details as we proceed.

Use short words to describe your job.

Your goal is to be understood, right?

Then avoid words like *liaises, interfaces, dialogues, transparencies, relationships, synergistic, stakeholders*. Replace them with short, simple, yet strong words, like **works, helps, builds, serves, makes, does, safety, improve, fix, protect, groups, people, concern**.

- ▶ Use short sentences and simple sentence structure.
- ▶ Simple words are far more powerful, and they are easier to remember.
- ▶ Simple sentences help prevent misquotes and are far easier to understand.

3. Write in the third person.

Why?

You are writing for someone else to read. Avoid *I, my* and *mine*. Use *he* or *she, his* or *her*.

Good spokespersons often refer to their organizations in the third person.

For example, instead of saying, "We're working to improve..," you might choose to start by saying "Big City Transit is working to improve..." You're referring to your organization here in the third person, like reporters do.

You're starting to write like a reporter. It's called **MediaSpeak.** It involves writing in news style the way journalists do.

News style involves writing in the third person, just as good news releases are prepared so that when you read them aloud, they sound like news stories.

When **your writing style** matches *news writing style*, the media is much more likely to use your defining words without changing them.

What will this message say?

Your introduction will include information that answers three basic questions about you:

Who you are, what you do and why you do it.

It will start with, "Our guest speaker today at _____(audience) is _____ (insert YOUR name here)."

If necessary, spell your name phonetically, for the introducer's benefit.

You can prepare a first, rough draft by jotting down key words or ideas that come to mind quickly. You might want to use a separate piece of paper for an outline, then adapt or edit the content into our final template.

You might include personal information that may be of general interest, such as a hobby or membership in an organization. It makes you interesting, but more importantly, it makes you look *human*.

Maybe you raise orphaned, personality-challenged dachshunds, you grow your own organic food, or you collect baseball cards.

A personal reference like this can become a great conversation starter after your presentation. You're making yourself look like a *real person* who might be interesting to listen to. And chances are if anyone raises the topic, you're ready, willing and able to talk about those items easily.

You decide what information you will want to use based on the makeup of each audience. There will always be a few people who will want to chat with you later about those unique topics, or will relate to you at that moment.

Include numbers, statistics or figures.

Why?

Facts, numbers and percentages add credibility to your message and make you look aware and informed. They make you look like a professional. We recommend you aim for three statistics to strengthen your message.

Example: "(Your name) works with 1,414 scientists from 249 healthcare organizations in 86 countries."

Avoid initials, acronyms and titles with too many words, but feel free to talk about some work you've done (or are doing) that makes you very proud.

We suggest you include something that makes you *personally unique,* or some accomplishment you're proud of. Maybe you were the first to win a certain award, you once worked on a famous project, or you were present when something big happened.

Mention some reasons why the audience should pay attention, or why your work is important to them, to you or to key publics.

Now that you've written down key bullet points or phrases, these become your core messages.

You may need little else in the way of a message. Some people learn to speak off the cuff from notes like these.

Closing Slogan

Close with a literary device, a motto, a figure of speech, slogan or cliché that sums up why you do what you do or why it is important. This may be difficult to choose for your first draft and you might change it later for each audience.

Examples:

▶ Tanya believes that better transit is up to everyone.

▶ Tom wants us to be part of the solution to making transit better.

▶ Terry can make it look as easy as one, two, three.

▷ **Tip:** If you're lost for a closing statement, find one in a good collection of quotations.

We like *The Oxford Dictionary of Phrase, Saying, and Quotation,* Oxford University Press, 1997.

Choose a topic from their list of themes, like **Speeches** on page 413.

The first quotation is from Cato the Elder, (234 - 149 BC) who said, ***"Grasp the subject, the words will follow."***

There's a lot of good writing and speaking advice in that quotation. You could write a book on that thought.

The One Minute Power Message Template

"Our guest speaker today at _____ is _____ .
(Name of audience) _(Your name)_

_____ works at (with, for, *etc.*) _____
(Your first name)

_____ .
(**Who** you are)

He/she recently _____

_____ .
(Something unique about you)

_____ 's job is to (make, do, work with, help, improve, *etc.*) _____
(Your first name)

_____

_____ .
(**What** you do, with 3 statistics)

The _____
(Issue or topic of your speech or message)

is important to _____ because _____
(Your first name)

_____

_____

_____ .
(**Why** you do what you do)

When it comes to the issue of _____ , _____
(Your first name)

believes in the old saying, _____

_____ .

Please join me in welcoming _____ ."
(Your name)

Please feel free to photocopy this page or share it with co-workers,
bosses, employees, friends.
We only ask that you make **quality** copies
and keep our company name on it.

www.neversaynocomment.com

Sample Notes for an introduction of Ian Taylor

Audience: College Public Relations Students. Toronto, Canada

Speech title: Never Say "NO COMMENT": How to answer tough questions.

Ian started by preparing a 3-it diagram and then wrote phrases containing both content and strategy. During his talk, he wanted to include some sales pitches for Toastmasters clubs and for his upcoming book.

Ian Taylor:

W h o : ▶ head of a communications specialty firm

▶ former public affairs manager, Toronto's Lester B. Pearson International Airport, has taught aviation managers from over 100 countries

▶ charter member, Rainbow Toastmasters (talk will include a plug for or recommendation to look at a nearby Toastmasters club)

W h a t : ▶ writes, speaks, trains, more than 10,000 students, 100 countries

▶ manages messages, issues and reputations

▶ students appear in news daily

W h y : ▶ help clients, students, others

▶ plug book, courses, speaking services (and website?)

▶ help you

Slogan:

Book title = motto = company name = website = speech title.

Now here's the introduction that Ian created from the above notes:

Introduction of Ian Taylor

Today's speaker heads a communications specialty firm called **Never Say "No Comment" Inc**.

Ian Taylor is the former public affairs manager at **Toronto's Lester B. Pearson International Airport**, and has taught aviation managers from over **100 countries.**

He's a charter member of **Rainbow Toastmasters** in Toronto.

Ian trains, consults and speaks about managing **messages, issues and reputations**.

He's trained over **10,000 students**, and is an official supplier to every level of government in this city.

Ian's students are in the news almost every day.

Ian believes there are some easy ways to stay out of trouble in interviews if you treat them like customer service encounters.

He's co-authored a **new book** on the topic and is here to give us a preview.

His company name, new book title, website and core message are all the same: Never Say "No Comment."

(pause)

Please join me in welcoming Ian Taylor.

(147 words in the body of this introduction)

Chapter 3

The One Minute Power Message — Part 2

Managing the Message:

Delivering it

Remembering it

Sticking to it — no matter what you're asked

Your next job is to read your own introduction out loud, just as someone else might read it for you.

Read it as it's written, with *no extras or embellishments*. It will probably feel a bit awkward at first.

Ask others to listen to your introduction, take notes, and then talk about what they remembered.

Ask them if the person who had been introduced sounded like an expert, sounded interesting, and whether there was something they might look forward to hearing the person talk about.

So, without looking back at the previous pages, answer the following questions:

What do you remember about Ian Taylor that makes him an expert?

What might you look forward to hearing Ian speak about?

What's his motto, slogan or saying?

We find that people usually remember the statistics: facts, figures or numbers. "Over 10,000 students, more than 100 countries, in the news every day."

They usually remember anything that was grouped into threes or had obvious literary structure, like: "Trains, consults and speaks; Message, issues and reputation management."

And they always remember his motto: **Never Say "No Comment"**

Another Introduction

Here's an advance look at one of our upcoming students of the future, Tom Lee.

You'll learn more about Tom and his job as we proceed into the year 2012.

For this introduction, Tom's audience is a high school auditorium filled with 800 students. He has a splashy *Powershow2010* presentation, because this group has a short attention span and can quickly become bored.

His goal is to convince students to participate in an interactive, online transit needs survey. He wants the students to go online, complete the survey, submit the information and possibly win big prizes.

This is a high school audience, one of the toughest. As noted, Tom has made a few changes in the order of his answers. You'll learn to do the same. There are no strict definitions to the system and lots of opportunities for flexibility in this method.

Our guest speaker today is Tom Lee from Big City Transit.

He's here to tell you how you could improve transit service and win a transit pass for life. *(This 'Why' statement has been moved to the beginning for impact.)*

Tom was an engineering professor at Big City University. *(Who?)*

In his spare time, he collects and trades baseball cards. *(Who?)*

Tom has worked to improve transit in Tokyo, London and Los Angeles. *(Who?)*

In those cities, a major priority was to improve transit service to schools. *(Who, what AND why?)*

Tom's working on a major program to examine every transit route in Big City. *(What?)*

That includes route 808 serving Hawthorne High.
(Aside: There might be some audience catcalls or a huge groan about now, discuss this with the introducer, so she/he can be ready.)

Students will be asked to fill out a detailed, online survey about your transit needs for new and better routes. *(What?)*

It's not only easy to do, it's fun, and Tom's here to show you how to **'Get on board'** and complete the survey. *(Why?)*

Would you please join me in welcoming our guest speaker, Tom Lee.

(149 words)

Now, answer these questions:

What do you remember about Tom Lee? (No fair peeking. Remember, this was an oral introduction. The audience only gets to hear it once, so you only get to read it once.)

What made him sound like an interesting expert?

What might you look forward to hearing him say if you were a student in the audience?

What's his slogan?

The answers to these questions are the small chunks of information your brain remembers after only hearing them said once as part of a larger presentation. They trigger something in our mind, and we remember even more of them when we take notes.

Previously, you probably remembered that Ian Taylor has taught more than 10,000 students from more than 100 countries.

You may have recalled he worked at Toronto's International Airport; maybe even it's name – Lester B. Pearson International, or that he's a member of Toastmasters – a charter member, no less – and perhaps even the colourful name of his club - Rainbow.

Or that he speaks about managing messages, issues and reputations, whatever that means.

You might want to hear him speak about those easy ways to stay out of trouble in an interview. If you were a public relations student, you'd probably want to learn how never to say "No comment."

Same thing for Tom.

You might have remembered he worked in 3 cities – *Tokyo, London and L.A.,* and that his job was to *improve* transit, especially student transit. The word "improve" was used three times in the introduction. Repetition increases retention.

Any baseball card fans in the audience are probably already on Tom's side, or will want to approach him after the presentation to chat. This small, personal touch makes Tom human.

His experience sure makes him sound like an expert.

You probably want to hear Tom say something about Bus Route 808 since you take it every day. And this survey thing – **"sounds like he really wants our input, but the real reason I'm gonna 'Get on Board' is 'cause, like, actually, I want to win big prizes!"**

Well, you get the picture.

These short, snappy answers to basic questions about who Ian (or Tom) is – what he does, maybe even why he does it – are really core messages, and if well crafted, they are also likely what a reporter would use as **sound bite** or a **quotable quote** in a news story.

Now, you get to meet **The Reporter From Hell**.

Some people call this **Not answering the question**.

It works like this. You are required to respond to each and every question the reporter asks by reading directly, word for word, from your introduction. You cannot **lie**. You cannot **deny**. And you can never say *"No comment."*

> ▶ You **must read** from your written notes when responding to the question.

▶ You **cannot improvise** your answers or embellish what's already written.

▶ You **cannot react** to the questions other than to read.

You'll get your first introduction to some control techniques you're encouraged to use, no matter how uncomfortable you feel at first.

▶ You may **pause** before answering the question—for as long as it takes to find a message to read from your introduction.

▶ You may ask the reporter to **repeat** or **clarify the question**.

▶ You may use a short **bridging phrase** such as "**Let me explain** what Tom is doing," or "**Let me tell you about** Tom's work today."

Here's how it would work with Tom's introduction:

 Reporter **F**rom **H**ell: "Is Tom here as part of some **glossy public relations** exercise to **cover up** bad transit? Why should we believe this guy?"

 Person **I**ntroducing **T**om: "Let me tell you why Tom's here." *[reads]* "Tom's **working** on a major program to examine every transit route in Big City. That includes Route 808 that serves **Hawthorne High**. He's here to tell the students how they could win a transit pass for life."

Doesn't sound like there's a cover up, does it?

 RFH: "So I suppose we got some academic, freeloading, out of touch bureaucrat here who's never done a thing of any good?"

 PIT: "Let me explain Tom's background. Tom has worked to **improve** transit in Tokyo, London and Los Angeles. In those cities, a major priority was to **improve** school transit."

Sounds like Tom's actually pretty experienced and he's there to help.

What would have happened if the response had been No comment?

 Reporter **F**rom **H**ell: "Is this part of some glossy public relations exercise to cover up bad transit?"

 Wrong Answer:
"No comment."

Sounds like there's a cover up of bad transit to us!

Trust us, folks, transit service is going to be getting much better, but maybe not until…

Chapter 4

Headline News

Imagine it's September 11, 2011.

Welcome to a fictional place called **Big City**.

The morning's news is filled with commemorative stories about the tragedies from a decade prior, now known simply as 9/11.

Your personal communicator prints out your daily newspaper on recycled paper.

You sit down for your simulated, reconstituted, coffee-type beverage and turn to the front page of the **Big City Bugle**.

There, you find a column by community champion Dennis Zonk, dealing with the tenth anniversary of 9/11.

His column tells us how things have changed.

Five Dollars
Weather: Ice Storms
and Floods.

Big City Bugle

September 11, 2011

10 Years that Changed our World

You've Been Zonked!
—by Dennis Zonk

Everywhere we look today, we'll be reminded of the events of 10 years ago.

We'll remember where we were and what we were doing when we heard the news that fateful morning.

We'll re-visit, however painfully, the images that have been etched forever on our memories by those twin towers.

We'll recall our individual attachments to the places and people of 9/11 and we'll grieve.

I can recall the four days I spent working in the South Tower of the World Trade Centre, just three months before it was brought down.

I knew people in that building.

I recall how their faces flashed back at me that morning ten years ago today.

I waited anxiously for a month before hearing that they all survived.

But let's mourn elsewhere and instead spend a moment here to look at what's happened since those fateful events.

It didn't take long after 9/11 for the political opportunists to come out of the woodwork.

Politicians tried to convince us that their war was about terrorism, but it didn't take long to find out what it was really about it was about power, money and energy. With a dose of 20th century corporate family values.

Politicians created a crisis and we got even.

It didn't take long to figure out who the true victims were in an energy war — we were.

You and I and every other energy consumer paid the price of that war, a war that fuelled the profits and lined the pockets of the corporate bullies.

You and I and other consumers fought back and we won the war.

The consumers took over. We forced our pension funds, our mutual funds and our financial institutions into backing publicly responsible corporations, often consumer-owned, consumer-managed and consumer-driven.

We did it with civil obedience, raw consumer action and boycotts as well.

Politicians created a crisis and we got even.

Governments over time tried every trick in the book to con us.

They under-funded public services of all types — until they could implement their strategy of create a crisis. It worked. For a while.

Politicians told us the only way to save public services was to privatize them to friends of these politicians. Talk about create a crisis!

Consumers finally had enough. We took over our own healthcare, education, and transit services first and we're on the verge of a new way of serving ourselves — untried, untested and unknown.

We got even with those politicians. We did away with the old boundaries and created new city states in a new world order unlike anything we might have imagined.

Oh, it was tough giving up our old city names and parochialisms.

Nobody liked the idea that they would live in Big City 74 or Big City 26, but we got used to it, barely.

The biggest change that's happened

Since 9/11 is, in my humble opinion, the advancement of what the

Ten years...

experts call issues groups.

They used to be called interest groups; then they became stakeholders. If you liked them.

If you didn't like them they were called special interest groups.

Soon they became known as issues groups, because we became so inter-connected through technology that we could use our consumer power and clout to get our way.

Our society has really evolved into three major issues groups: the corporate world, the consumer world and the self-employed world.

Unions have largely disappeared as good workers sought self-employment contracts from their employers.

So, in 10 years, things have really changed. We've come a long, long way.

We were hit, we fell down, now we're getting up in an all-new way.

Remember, I'll be here on your side, keeping an eye out for mismanagement wherever we find it.

Usually, in this space, we Zonk some incompetent manager somewhere, but today is different. There's no Zonk attack today, folks; instead, give yourself a pat on the back.

But don't forget our motto: snitch on your manager today. Report mismanagement everywhere. You know how to reach me.

Chapter 5

Welcome To 2012 And A Place Called Big City

Looking at Big City Transit

Seeing the challenges facing transit services

Introducing our first student

The Big City region covers over 22,000 square kilometres, somewhere in the continent formerly known as North America. It is an amalgamation of 7 former large cities, with a combined population of over 14 million people. They are in urgent need of immediate improvements in public transportation. Estimates place the cost of upgrading the transit system at nearly twenty billion dollars.

The amalgamated city-state takes in 7 separate urban transit systems, 4 airports, 14 toll bridges or tunnels, 28 tolled highways and three ports under a new umbrella agency, Big City Transit or, as it's now known, BCT.

BCT operates subways, streetcars, buses, trolleys, light rail transit, the taxi and limousine system, the share-a-car service and the share-a-bike service. Not to mention the trucking system and all rail services. They are within a year of achieving a system that runs on time.

There is no shortage of management skills to do the job right. Good managers have kept these systems running despite the ineptitude of their former political and corporate bosses.

Finally, managers are being allowed to manage a transportation system with a wealth of potential, and they are doing it by working directly with transportation users – a novel idea if there ever was one.

In planning transit in the past, there had been an array of hub and spoke systems to serve the individual needs of the former city boundaries. As a result, the best hubs didn't always connect well with the best spokes in the larger city, based on actual need and potential usage.

Meet Tom Lee.

Big City Transit has brought together public, semi-public and private transportation systems into a new super-agency, and Tom Lee might just be one of the people to help make it super.

Tom's expertise is in creating simulations for new transit systems. He shows them how to connect a university's transit needs with the transit needs of a nearby factory, shopping mall or amusement park. Often these facilities operate on different demand periods so any new transit system must have major flexibility in its routes and scheduling.

Tom's job is to examine the transit needs of the entire Big City and bring in new schedules and innovative routes that will increase ridership, better serve the large suburban destinations, and make greater use of new and existing transit equipment.

He worked on similar projects in Big Cities formerly known as Tokyo, London and Los Angeles, and met with some success. Now he hopes to repeat that success in this Big City, with the direct involvement of transit users.

Public consultation is to be truly consultative – the transit users will make the decisions for their transit system by completing online ridership needs surveys.

Building a business-like relationship with the news media will be essential. That's one reason Tom was privately enrolled at Big City's Institute for Serving the Public's Information Needs, or SPIN College, as it's known.

Tom's main job will be to initiate widespread public consultation with community groups, businesses and transit-users. He is working toward a radical new system of routes and schedules that requires public support to succeed.

Any major route changes will also require cooperation from major urban employers, developers and institutions of all types.

Businesses might need to re-examine hours of operation.

Companies might need to build new on-site transit terminals or specialized parking lots.

Some employers might provide direct financial support for new services as a way to encourage employees to take transit. They might provide employees with free transit passes. Everyone was being encouraged to participate in the transit planning process.

Tom's work is part of a three-stage improvement plan for transit.

Once the new schedules and routes have been developed, a second team of experts will examine transit equipment needs, then a third team will examine fares and user fees. The teams will then combine their findings into a recommended plan for Big City Transit's new, incoming board of directors for final approval.

Tom knew fares would be the most controversial step in making changes. There are some who want full cost-recovery at the fare box, while others want a no-fee transit system.

The fare issue has always threatened the success of the consultations into schedules and routes, so Tom's goal is to *manage the message* around schedules and routes issues only.

Tom has heard various rumours about transit fares, including a radical new no-fare policy, but he knows he can't comment on fares. Tom is at SPIN College to learn to manage his message, his issues and his reputation without saying "No comment."

The training sessions at SPIN College involve role-playing, and Tom is a bit unhappy at the idea.

Part of him thinks he's already an expert at dealing with the news media. After all, he was recently featured in the **Big City Press** as an up and comer in transportation planning. It was a full-page story in the People section and included colour photographs of transit models Tom had designed for the cities formerly known as London, Tokyo and Los Angeles.

A SPIN College instructor told Tom the earlier news article was a puff piece, a one-sided, non-controversial news item on Tom's software applications, with no critics or opposing viewpoints. She told Tom that most news had some element of controversy and all news had a potential for controversy. She said he should expect to encounter more controversy with this assignment.

"How could there be any controversy in my work now?" Tom wondered, innocently.

He didn't really think he had too much to learn; after all, he had been a university lecturer and had written dozens of technical articles, so he considered himself an expert communicator. The articles appeared in international engineering publications and websites, and were widely read by senior engineering students and academics all over the world.

The instructor carefully explained the opening scenario. SPIN College officials called it the *humility experience*. The students called it meeting the *reporter from hell.*

For his opening assignment, Tom was to deliver a prepared speech, and then answer some questions from a computer-simulated audience. Then he would face an instructor playing the role of a reporter, impersonating Dennis Zonk.

Zonk was a weekly city columnist and sometime transportation reporter at the **Big City Bugle**, a feisty tabloid newspaper famous for its outrageous stunts and sex-trade advertisements.

Zonk's column was called *You've been Zonked!*

It set out to embarrass **mismanagers**, some of whom had been fired, not always because of mismanagement, but because of making mistakes in the news media. Tom was sure he could survive a Zonk encounter.

Ian Taylor, the founder of SPIN College, played the role of Dennis Zonk.

No one knew what Dennis Zonk really looked like *(his face never appeared in his columns),* but the founder looked intimidating. Ian could frighten people, anger them, or pretend to act very confused—even when he wasn't role-playing.

The speech part was easy. Tom's One Minute Power Message was used to set him up to succeed with his audience. Then, he simply had to read his prepared text. He'd managed to deliver it fairly well, he thought.

It was very easy to read. Tom wondered who had written it. The writer had obviously employed a certain style of word-crafting that was very conversational.

The words were short, as were the sentences.

Each sentence was a paragraph in length, and typed in large serif font that was easy to read.

Tom knew that, under pressure, he could sound too much like an academic. It was his natural defence mechanism to talk like a textbook, and he hoped he could learn ways to deal with it.

The day's specially prepared speech text included sample answers for him to use, and they were written in the same simple, conversational style. Tom liked the way the writer had summed up his task for him and he knew he would want to borrow large parts of this speech for his own adaptation and later use.

Tom would later go on to become an expert editor, based on the skills he learned at SPIN College. His Aunt Betty later told him he had become a spin doctor. She found nothing wrong with that, she pointed out, since she'd always wanted a nephew who was a doctor.

In the opening words of the prepared speech, Tom explained that once new schedules and routes had been developed, work could begin on the equipment needs, and then finally the fare issue.

First of all, however, detailed, thorough and comprehensive talks were to take place on things such as changes in working hours and employee scheduling, new transit access points and on-company parking for transit equipment, and new services and routes that had previously never even been considered. All of this information would be gathered electronically, through Tom's new computer system.

Tom's speech had a checklist of ideas and tasks and he found himself delivering his message with more enthusiasm than he ever had. The words gave him a lot of new insight and turned him on to the opportunities. His simulated audience gave him remarkable feedback. Even if they were simulated, they seemed stimulated.

Next, he fielded questions from the 97 representatives in the *cyber videoconference* and he managed to stick to his prepared notes. In fact, he'd felt comfortable with the words, and the comfort had flown through him to his audience. All of the questions were technical or operational and Tom answered them with ease.

Tom realized that in order to comfort an audience, one had to look comfortable. If you looked uncomfortable, people tended to think you were guilty of something.

Following the questions and answers, he was to walk over to the lounge where he would meet the reporter/columnist to answer a few questions.

Tom figured this would be easy. Since the topic of scheduling was so important, he'd have the old-time reporter eating out of his hand. Nothing was ever as easy as it seems, as they say.

Tom walked down the hall to the lounge. As he walked in, he noticed an older man filling a cup with reconstituted, simulated, coffee-type beverage product. Tom's humility exercise was about to start, as he came face to face with *the reporter from hell*.

Chapter 6

Tom Meets The Reporter From Hell

Ambush questions

Failure to negotiate

Saying "No comment"

"You Tom Lee?" the man impersonating *Dennis Zonk* asked gruffly, without even turning to look at Tom.

Before Tom could answer, the reporter-impersonator continued, "So I hear you got some secret plan to bring in major fare increases. Do you deny it?"

"I can assure you there's no such secret plan." Tom said as he wrinkled his face, frowned and stepped back from the man. He was wondering how this interview might get started officially.

For good measure, he threw in, "I have **no comment** about any secret plan."

"What will this secret plan do to retired people and the poor – are you going to make them hitchhike to get around?"

"No comment," said Tom.

"So, can you guarantee there won't be fare gouging to pad the pockets of special interests?"

"There are no guarantees in life; everyone knows that, I'm sure."

"So, a huge fare increase **is** possible. How bad could it be?"

"Well. I suppose that technically, anything's possible in the future. Besides, that's not my department."

This guy was getting on Tom's nerves and he hoped the *formal interview* would be more polite.

Zonk didn't miss a beat. He almost snarled when he asked, "Have you got any orders from the Mayor not to talk about this?"

Tom just had to set this guy straight. "No, of course not. I don't report to the Mayor. I…"

Without giving Tom time to finish, the reporter barged ahead.

"Do you deny that there's a hidden agenda to skyrocket fares to cover the new transit headquarters cost overruns?"

"No way is that true. There's no hidden agenda here," Tom replied. *Where was this guy getting all this stuff?*

"Come on, everyone knows this so-called public consultation of yours is nothing more than a clever smokescreen to hide the political damage created by the Mayor's old pals on the transit board. Isn't this just a way to cover up a crisis that threatens to destroy public transit in Big City? In your opinion, Mr. Lee, is the mayor a moron for taking this position?"

"No comment," he insisted. He didn't want the reporter to quote him talking about any of this stuff.

He was starting to catch on, he thought.

Wrongly.

He figured saying "No comment" would end this line of questioning. He knew he had to get this interview started right.

"Now, where should we go for this interview?" Tom asked.

"Oh, I already have enough for a news story," the reporter remarked. "I don't have any more questions, thank you."

And with that, the man impersonating *Dennis Zonk* shuffled out of the room leaving Tom wondering what was going on.

This had seemed so unprofessional that Tom wondered whether this was even like a real encounter. He felt like he'd been run over by a *fire truck*.

Chapter 7

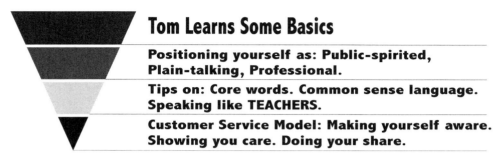

Tom Learns Some Basics

Positioning yourself as: Public-spirited, Plain-talking, Professional.

Tips on: Core words. Common sense language. Speaking like TEACHERS.

Customer Service Model: Making yourself aware. Showing you care. Doing your share.

A SPIN College instructor entered the room and told Tom that the analysis of his interview would take place in about two hours.

"In the meantime, Mr. Lee, would you mind sitting in on an opening lecture that's just about to start in the main theatre? This will give you some background and overview of our approach to your training," she said.

Tom, still a bit stunned from his Zonk encounter, arrived just as the lecture was starting. He noticed several managers from Big City Transit in the classroom, as well as several engineers he recognized from the transportation community in Big City.

The following is a transcript of the opening lecture, which Tom recorded on his personal communicator, a device that combined a telephone, camera, personal computer, identifier and much more. Every citizen had one.

The Opening Lecture:

Good morning everyone. Thank you for being here.

Welcome to the *Institute for Serving the Public's Information Needs*. I'd like to say how pleased we are that you could join us for the next few days. We especially want to welcome those of you joining us for the first time. Don't worry; we'll be gentle. *(Laughter)*

We're going to teach you a lot of theory over the next few days, but we'll do it with examples of how the theory is applied to situations like yours.

In order to do that, we're going to recommend some suggested messages to serve as examples of our methods.

They are suggestions only. You should always, always, always contact your communications department before agreeing to any media encounter and for information and advice or direction on your organization's *official messages.*

This is our advice only; you are not being directed to do anything. Direction is different from advice.

Remember that the final decision on your messages will be up to you and your organization.

Over the next few days, we're going to be talking about three broad areas — *developing your message, defining your message and delivering your message,* as shown in these diagrams:

Developing your message includes 3 major components:

Positioning yourself, your audience and your issues

Relationships, including motivation, key publics and dealing with bosses

Communications strategies for you (or your organization)

Defining your message is all about:

Choosing the right words and phrases

Structuring them for the spoken word

Packaging them into the right formats for effective delivery

Delivering your message is about:

Avoiding the traps of negative messaging

Structuring your core messages into quotable quotes

Speaking style and presentation skills

We'll look at the concept of negative messaging:

▶ How reporters try to define an issue negatively

▶ How to replace negative words by disproving them

▶ Why you should never say "No comment."

And you'll learn how to choose the best words for your message:

▶ Words that just make common sense

▶ The inarguable premise

▶ The Spin Doctor's Game

Then we'll teach you how to package those words into what we call *pillars, supports and sparklers,* including our own 3-it method, which we've used in these diagrams. You'll learn the theory as we apply it to your issues during your training here.

How do we know what someone's position is on an issue?

By the words they use to describe their position, combined with the actions they take, and the final perception of those words and actions by the rest of the public.

How do we define an issue?

With words. If we call a situation a crisis, we're defining the issue as a crisis.

Others may or may not agree and have different words to describe it.

If we call the situation an opportunity, we've changed the perception significantly. We've gone from one extreme to the other, and maybe the truth is in the middle somewhere.

Our messages contribute to how the issue becomes defined by the public, often through the news media or other media.

We have to position ourselves in this process – sometimes we position ourselves at the extremes of the issues, but more often we're somewhere in between those extremes. When you know what words are most acceptable to your target public(s) you can position yourself on their side of the issue – *the right side*.

Positioning yourself on the right side of an issue

The goal of good messaging involves positioning yourself on the right side of an issue.

You'll notice we've carefully avoided the words *positive* or *popular*. We prefer the tongue-twister.

Positioning yourself as:

▶▶ **Public-spirited**

▶▶ **Plain-talking**

▶▶ **Professional**

Let's start with the concept of being public-spirited.

It means positioning what you're doing or saying in the interests of the public, or in the interests of your most important audience(s).

Maybe an unpopular plant closure is best for the stockholders and the long-term interests of the company, no matter how the closure might destroy the lives of workers. Lots of people will take different positions on this kind of issue and each might use different words to define and describe how they feel. Unemployed workers, real estate agents and area politicians will define the closure differently, using words that suit their self-interest.

Let's look at some issues as seen in various headlines or lead sentences – whether they're from a corporate news release or a newspaper article or broadcast piece or simply the first part of your core message.

Here are two very different news messages involving spin:

Businesses employing less than 30 workers can expect to benefit from tax changes being proposed today by the Mayor's Task Force on Tax Reduction.

The other message begins:

Big City Mayor, The Honourable Melissa W. Daley, LLB, PHD, today proudly announced the release of the Mayor's Task Force on Tax Reduction...

Which message is more public-spirited?

One of the messages serves the needs of small businesses, their workers and their families. The other serves the political needs of the Mayor.

Obviously the second message is clearly motivated by the political interests of the Mayor and would be re-written by a responsible news editor.

Which message would best serve the broadest public interest in such an issue? Which one do you think the news media might choose? Which one might get changed?

Which one is written in news style, or **MediaSpeak***, and which one is written in what we call **PRspeak**?

PRspeak contains too many superlatives, is too positive to believe, and generally places the corporate interests ahead of the public's interests. It's often prepared to satisfy or please the client, and newsrooms hate it. It's light on facts and heavy on *"fabulous."*

Our next examples are possible corporate messages from Big City Utility Services. The first one begins:

---

*For more details on the theory of MediaSpeak and all about pillars, supports and sparklers, check out Ian Taylor's 1999 textbook, *MediaSpeak: The bold New Guide to Public Relations and Reputation Management*. (www.neversaynocomment.com)

Homeowners should check for water damage as a result of recent record downpours. An office has been set up to help...

The other:

City water officials were quick to react to last month's record flooding due to water-main breaks.

Self-praise is almost always seen as faint praise. Let somebody else say that you were quick to react. This second message is a bit too self-congratulatory for you to use when talking about yourself.

Excellence should never be self-declared.
It should be displayed.
— *Ian Taylor*

Now, let's look at how different news stories might appear, based on placing a different spin on the various players involved. Here's an example of MediaSpeak wording:

Drivers are being warned to slow down for construction on a stretch of highway responsible for three deaths recently.

Asphalt repairs are underway along Waterfront Highway between Dominion Ave. and Main Street.

Just last week, eighteen children died when a speeding motorist...

Compare that to this PRspeak:

Police Chief Big Ego declared war on speeders today at a special unveiling of his 2012 budget at City Hall.

He demanded more funding for traffic enforcement, another three helicopters, along with another 1,200 male police officers.

While denying any political aspirations, Chief Big Ego stressed his record in reducing jaywalking.

When you position your message in the interests of your publics, you move the focus away from yourself. You are seen to be acting for your customers, for your shareholders, for future generations, or for the community. Your message builds a bond between you and those publics. You become almost an advocate for your publics — a true professional.

> ▷ **Tip:** You'll want to be very careful when using the **I** word, *unless you want to make yourself a target in the issue.* Remember the introduction exercise, written in the third person.
>
> You might choose to talk about **we**, but better yet the third person. For example:
>
> "**Big City Transit** is working to…"
>
> This is a strategic effort, positioning you as a describer, explainer or informer, rather than as a defensive, reactive spokesperson.

Plain Talk

George Orwell once said: "Plain language is the enemy of insincerity."

If you truly care about the recipients of your message, you'll speak to them in plain talk, with easy to understand examples and simple phrases that will drive home your points.

Plain talk is the essence of common sense language.

If you'll recall, around the turn of the 21st century, folks were quick to blame a lot of our problems on big government and uncaring bureaucrats. The result was the creation of new city-states that were consumer-driven.

Public servants in the past were poorly prepared to respond to criticism of any type, because they were often muzzled or forced to dispense messages that were poorly prepared, filled with jargon, buzzwords and bureaucratized language. There were too many answers that amounted to *"It's not my department."*

It often seemed that the bureaucrats were out of touch and clearly they were seen as the main part of the problem. Most bureaucrats couldn't speak like ordinary people, but spoke a foreign language from a culture few could identify with.

Bureaucrats were often instructed or **ordered to deny** there was a problem, even when they knew there were problems in the public sector.

They were told to issue false assurances that improvements were being made in public services. Often, however, they seemed to display no knowledge of the larger issues that people cared about.

Politicians were quick to ridicule the bureaucracy and news rooms were loath to speak to a bureaucrat, except when they wanted to show the world how out of touch that bureaucrat was.

Examples of BureaucratSpeak (and what it really means):

We're facilitating the kinds of interrelationships to create synergistic transparencies in dialoguing with a multitude of stakeholders which will most likely and quite possibly even lead to opportunities for greater discussions towards mutually acceptable terms of reference. **(We hope somebody else has a clue, because we sure don't.)**

Taking into account the previous factors heretofore mentioned, and assuming a continuation of the current state of relationships, this effort at creating dialogue may result in a move toward some fundamental understanding of the various synergistic interrelationships, which will create the appropriate forum for stakeholder enlightenment. **(We're waiting for something to do.)**

We can assure you we're undertaking the best work possible taking into account the present administrative and fiscal environment and resource situation, and given the present uncertainty about possible future financial factors outside our sphere of influence. **(We're at a standstill because we're broke and confused.)**

Feel free to send your favourite examples to:
spindoc@neversaynocomment.com You might win prizes.

What went wrong?

Public messages ranged from mumbling BureaucratSpeak to unbelievable PRSpeak, instead of relying on the basic plain-talk principles of MediaSpeak.

Corporate interests became the priority, instead of appealing to the public interest. The messages were so dense that few would believe them. They were not written in news style, but in a style few could understand or relate to.

The BureaucratSpeak messages became sanitized, dull, boring and contained no news of any value to anyone. They looked like a committee had written them.

They were poorly written for oral or spoken delivery. (One government media message we studied had 32 pages of background material, and 46 words of message. It should be the other way around, folks.)

The messages often went above people's heads (too technical or poor vocabulary) or spoke down to the public. They were filled with *euphemisms, buzzwords and catchphrases* that real people didn't understand.

The messages were either filled with qualifiers and run-on sentences or else they amounted to "Trust us; we're facilitating a solution expeditiously." People started to think, *"Yeah, sure."*

Or worse yet, bureaucrats were ordered to say, "We're doing the best we can with the resources available." It was seldom seen as being good enough, nor did anyone believe it without proof. *The statement was highly arguable.* What was missing was **plain talk**.

> ▷ **Tip:** Read what you can by Rudolf Flesch, author of *How to write, speak and think more effectively,* and several other important texts.
>
> Flesch designed the readability quotient, which calculates reading and comprehension levels.
>
> Computer word processing software has several programs to help you prepare your messages in plain talk.
>
> The technology quickly tells us what grade level is required for the reader to understand our message.
>
> We once saw a bureaucratic document, a so-called media line requiring a grade 18 level of education to be understood. It did not serve the public's needs. Nor the needs of the poor spokesperson, who really could have used some common sense language.

Only in about 2010, when bureaucrats started to speak like elementary school teachers, did the public gain a better understanding of the issues. The teacher-as-spokesperson model is based on plain talk, developed at SPIN College.

Think of all the important people in your lives and chances are they were plain-talking folks. Chances are we can recall a relative, neighbour, friend or mentor who had that special gift of cutting through the crap, summing things up and finding a way to deal with it all in a message that just made common sense.

Now, in 2012, plain talk has become pervasive. Since 2009, companies with computer help desks have only been hiring people who can speak in plain talk. This is real progress.

The essence of plain talk is: short words, short sentences, short paragraphs. Never use a 50 cent word when a five cent word will do. After all, terms like *consulting with, dialoguing, interfacing, interacting or liasing* all mean **talk**.

SPIN College's core words for bureaucrats

If you're a public sector worker or middle manager in a large organization, many people will automatically assume you're lazy, out of touch or uncaring.

Do you want a reputation as a *bungling bureaucrat* or as a *professional public servant* ? Choose the spin you'd like to achieve for your reputation.

What are the shortest, most effective words to influence or improve your reputation for public-spirited action, plain talk and professionalism?

The answer: words like *work,* (you cannot over-use the word work) *help, build, safe, protect, care, serve* and *save*. Not a complete list, but a start.

Some other important one-syllable words in displaying professionalism: *fix, team, plan, grow, health, talk, hear, do, you, your*.

> ▷ **Tip:** Try to write or speak a line and just use words with one beat in them. It is quite hard. Try to write a whole book in the same way and you'll see what I mean. But, know this one thing: one beat words work best for you and for those who hear you.

Common sense language

▮▸ **Common sense** language is often rooted in sacred beliefs such as standing up for our communities, our country or what we hold near and dear.

▮▸ **Common sense** language can include phrases like working together, *working for what's important, making our communities safe from criminals,* or *giving people a hand-up and not a hand-out*. It's about *working to help, working to improve, working to build*.

▮▸ **Common sense** language is about putting issues into simple language and linking them to the greater issue of the public good.

Your new messages will consist of short words, short sentences and tight writing skills.

When your message is meant to speak to the public, you must learn to write words that are *designed to be spoken to an audience, out loud.*

A lot of writing is prepared to be read silently from a page or screen. As a result, we're losing our oratorical writing skills, skills that call for simplicity, clarity and brevity in the spoken word.

It's never easy to keep it simple.

It can take longer to prepare a short message than a long one. Mark Twain claimed it took him three days to write a good ad-lib. At SPIN college, we've taken weeks, or sometimes only seconds to come up with that *just-right sound-bite or quotable quote.*

A 30 page message prepared two weeks after an issue breaks is not as effective as a 30 word message prepared within the first minutes of the issue making the news.

Make a personal commitment to plain talk, or spend your career sounding, acting and looking like a bureaucrat. The choice is yours.

Professionalism

There's a word we don't hear too often these days.

Picture some of the most important professionals in your life – *your favourite teacher, a health professional, a mentor.* What makes them good at what they do? Chances are they're good common sense communicators, and you can learn a lot from them.

Professionalism is often about appearances — about looking like you know what the heck you're doing in times of trouble or when you're under pressure.

It can start when you enter a room to speak: stride purposefully to the platform and take your place at the lectern. Before you've said a word, you will have displayed a degree of professionalism in your body language, eye contact, apparel and appearance. It's far more than just image, however. It's about the total message.

Being professional is about being a good *explainer, describer* and *informer.* It's about avoiding defensiveness, negative reactions and the traps of a communications encounter by letting your professionalism shine through.

Here are three factors that influence your display of professionalism in the spoken word:

1. Crisis management communications

When a problem arises, you'll know how to proceed in an orderly manner, like an expert. Whether you're investigating a crime scene, dealing with a natural disaster or suddenly faced with a hostile situation, the core communications message is similar.

You need to let people know that: **you're assessing the situation** in a step-by-step manner; **you're setting clear priorities**; and **you have a team, a plan and specific resources** to handle the situation, (or you're working at getting them).

That's the most basic messaging approach to almost any crisis or incident – the SPIN College Crisis Communications Model.

You can change the wording if you wish, but this simple three-step plan can form the basis of a crisis communications statement for many situations you'll face.

2. Use of facts, statistics, research

One of the most basic ways to show someone you're smart is to rattle off some key numbers. Almost all public issues have their roots in analysis of statistics and research. Invariably, a story will be driven by its key numbers.

It's not enough to say you're working with community groups. It's important to point out, for example, that you've met with 37 community organizations at over 50 public meetings attended by over 2,200 people.

Why would you just say you've got staff working on a situation, when you could say you've assigned 4 officers to the task, supported by 6 workers from this agency, 3 from that agency and 7 from another agency, naming each specific agency.

Professionalism is like excellence. One shouldn't declare one's professionalism – few will believe you if you haven't proven it. Instead, one should display one's professionalism through your presentation. Facts, key numbers, data, amounts, percentages and other *factoids* go a long way to prove you're informed and proceeding with professionalism.

Take the issue of resource or staffing levels — please. If you say publicly that you have enough resources or staff, you won't likely ever get any more. If you publicly say you don't have enough staff you may be seen to be critical of your organization's decision-making.

If you need more staff, your message might focus on:

> ▶ the existing staff levels, compared to a few years ago,
> ▶ the impact of any changes in staffing or steps taken to improve efficiencies of staff, and
> ▶ any steps that are being taken or need to be taken to address staffing concerns in the future.

Let the recipient of the message decide if you have enough resources, based on your presentation of the facts, the situation and the impact.

3. For instances

Reporters and audiences love them and they're the most important teaching and explaining tool we know.

They're case studies, examples, detailed background items. These are what we call **sparklers** and you'll see lots of them at Spin College.

Consider the question: *"Are you doing enough to deal with the issue of neighbourhood safety?"*

You might choose to answer a question by detailing the work you've done, followed by an example, or sparkler.

Example:

"We're working to improve neighbourhood security.

"For instance, for the past 12 years, we've been working with 36 community groups to reduce crime.

"It's a unique twist on the **Neighbourhood Watch program** *involving over 200 volunteers.*

"We've added video security monitoring on several streets where crime levels were high.

"By working with the police, there's been a reduction in crime rates of over 15 percent.

"That's real progress."

What if you're asked if you have enough equipment to deal with a massive winter ice storm?

Why just say you have enough equipment, when you can provide a detailed synopsis of the number of pieces of equipment, list some of the special features of that equipment and give an example of how the public will benefit from the use of that equipment.

You might talk about the costs, or the savings achieved, or the three main benefits of a new procedure, or method of operating. This helps the receiver of the message create a visual image of you as a professional subject matter expert.

Good examples are like great photo opportunities—a picture is worth a thousand words and a good for instance tells a lot of story by itself. Good storytellers make great spokespersons.

In the world of sales and marketing, examples are known as **proof statements**. It's not enough to say that something is good. An example can display goodness.

Good spokespersons are good TEACHERS

Tact. If you want to inflame an issue, use inflammatory language. If you want to be controversial, make controversial statements. If you want to control an issue, control your language. Tact can help you control controversy.

Elocution. Speak clearly. Read a news story out loud from this morning's newspaper. Emphasize, even o-ver-em-pha-size, the final consonant in each word. This technique is used by news-readers to keep their consonants crisp. Crisp would sound like *Crispuh!*

Articulation. To be well-spoken, interesting, easy to listen to. Express yourself clearly in order to make complex things easy to understand. Bring things to life so that what you're saying just makes common sense.

Candour. Be open when things go wrong. Avoid being defensive with phrases like, *Well, I can assure you, we're doing the best we can.* Or, *That's not my department.* Instead, admit when there have been some problems, say you're sorry, and explain how you're fixing the problems.

Humantiy. Remember our first priority – place the issue in the public interest. Every issue is, at its roots, a people issue. Picture your audiences and develop messages that will serve their information needs.

Enthusiasm. There's no business like show business. So keep on smiling. Even when you're tired and you've been delivering the same message for days, make the next encounter just as fresh and spontaneous as your first one. TV especially demands a certain degree of perkiness, liveliness, and enthusiasm. Smiling helps add comfort to your message.

Research. Use facts, numbers, statistics, comparisons, percentages, polls, research, focus groups, study data. Make sure they're accurate, and very carefully selected.

Strategies. You should have clear communications objectives tied to your public's needs and your organization's priorities. Your goal may be to sell products, increase donations or just keep your job. Likely you'll have three major goals, right?

As spokespersons, we're here to inform people, to fulfill one of the most important jobs in an information-rich society. Good spokespersons are always good teachers.

Good teaching gives students the skills to succeed. Now let's combine teaching skills with customer service skills.

Treating the Public Like Customers—Understanding the Message Recipient

What does the message recipient want to hear? Invariably, they want to hear that there's somebody out there protecting their interests and taking care of things that might affect them. They want to hear that everything's fine, but it's not enough just to say everything's fine.

Let's look at the message recipients as we would if they were customers.

As customers in a store, they may need to find someone who knows where things are, who cares about their needs and who will do what they can to help them.

Here's one of the easiest message models you'll ever find. It's the **SPIN College Customer Service Communications Model**, and naturally, it consists of three parts.

SPIN College Customer Service Communications Model:

Being aware

Showing you care

Doing your share

Being Aware (or Becoming Aware)

Here at SPIN College, we have detailed profiles on the many issues groups you'll be dealing with, as well as some *backgrounders* on the movers and shakers in Big City.

Awareness starts with a thorough understanding of your key publics, clients, audiences, issues groups or customers. It's about knowing what concerns them, what motivates them and, most importantly, what their needs are.

To prove you're aware of an issue, your message must describe and define the issue from the publics' or customers' perspective. Your message often requires a re-stating of the essentials, with the clever use of facts, figures, statistics, research, and examples.

Re-stating the essential facts around an issue can serve as your essential core message, even as decisions about resolving an issue are being made. It makes you look like a teacher.

Making yourself aware of issues can be time-consuming and it's hard work. It involves research, study and analysis. It can involve media monitoring, public opinion analysis, trends research and access to a wealth of information. New technology makes much of the work easier. Our files are at your disposal.

Awareness is gained in front-line communication. That means you'll be getting out and listening to real people in real situations, asking them the right questions and hearing their concerns in every opportunity available to you. Some call this *management by walking around,* or, when done poorly, *management by wandering aimlessly.*

Now, what does saying "No comment" reveal about your awareness of an issue? When you say "No comment," you've missed an opportunity to show that you are at least aware of the situation. Instead, you could simply say, "Yes, we've just learned of the accident. We're anxious to know…"

> Cindy Jean Cregg, press secretary to the best President the United States of America never had, once said that information creates confidence, while silence breeds fear.

Awareness is a strategic element, and everyone wants it today. We're an information-rich society and we expect instant answers. There are high levels of accountability today, unlike a few years ago.

You may need to buy time on your issues, to defer the question until more information becomes available. After all, in managing a message in a sudden situation, you start by assessing the situation, then making yourself aware before communicating with your key publics.

What happens when you're not aware of what's going on?

In a news encounter, the reporter is the medium or the vessel that takes your message to your customer. You need to make yourself aware of the reporter's and the public's needs and concerns quickly.

When you're faced with an angry reporter (or public or customer), you need to be aware of what caused the anger before you can do anything to help.

One of the most effective ways of calming down an angry person is to ask soft, open style questions. Here are a few:

> *Can you tell me exactly what happened, please?*
> *Could you be a bit more specific, please?*
> *When or where did this happen?*
> *What can I do to help you?*
> *May I take a few moments to get that information for you?*

A "No comment" response would emphasize your lack of awareness—to your customers, to your publics, to your audience.

Often, awareness is simply about spoken acknowledgement that there's a problem.

We need to recognize that fear may be a silent, hidden, and major motivator.

Fear must be identified and acknowledged somehow in your messages, even if the simple message is, "Yes, there is some concern over the future of fares for public transit, that's why we're working to establish a new route system first."

Showing you Care

Saying "No comment" is like saying you don't care—about your customers, your audience, your publics. If you want to be perceived as being on their side, you'd better be able to show you care about what they care about.

The word care is interchangeable with concern. (Concern just didn't rhyme.)

> ▷ **Tip:** Never let anyone else **out-concern** you on an issue.

If someone is suddenly interested in your project costs, to suggest that cost is not important right now is argumentative. Did you want to start an argument already? You come across as not caring about other people's money.

Remember your opening writing exercise — your introduction? Your **why** statements are your **care** statements. You care enough to do something. Or, because you care, you're asking the public to do things to help you. That's how you create inarguability. Who can argue with doing our part to improve transit?

"The (issue or topic of your speech or message) is important to _____ (your first name) because ..." followed by three examples or reasons why you do what you do:

> *"Costs are important to Big City Transit. That's why we looked for savings in better transit routes and schedules; that's why we broadened our advertising base; and that's why we started partnership promotions like the one with Hawthorne High."*

Doing Your Share

When you can't do it all, you can at least do your share. When you can't care about everything, you can care about your share of the responsibilities.

Your role statement is one of your most essential messages. We'll help you write them.

Remember that if you're the evening's musical director, it's not your job to cook the food. You can refer complaints or compliments about food to the chef.

Remember the old poem, author unknown, with apologies for memory lapses.

> *It's not my job to run the train, the schedule I don't know.*
> *It's not for me to say how far the train's allowed to go.*
> *I cannot blow the whistle. I must not ring the bell.*
> *But let the damn thing jump the tracks and see who catches hell.*

Or, as re-written at SPIN College:

> *But when it finally jumps the tracks, I'll meet the* **Reporter From Hell***.*

Doing your share messages tell your audience what it is that you are doing, what part of the task is your responsibility and what part of the task is someone else's.

▷ **Tip:** When talking about your partners, refer to them specifically by name. Rather than say you're working with the police, say, *"We're working with the Big City Police Department."* Rather than say you're working with businesses, say, *"We're working with the Big City Board of Trade and 44 businesses in the retail and service sector, including Happy's, StallMart, and Shoppers Appliances."*

The specific reference to your partners allows you to display your professionalism while basking in the reputations of your partners.

If you say "No comment," you're telling your customers, your audience, your publics that you aren't aware, don't care and you're refusing to do your share.

So, students, this concludes our opening lecture. We'll answer some questions, and then take a break so that you can return to your instructors for some feedback on your opening assignments.

Chapter 8

Headline News

Five Dollars
Weather: Gloomy
with ice storms.

Big City Bugle

May 27, 2012

Transit denies secret agenda to skyrocket fares

Mayor not covering up, Transit official says

You've been Zonked!
—by Dennis Zonk

A senior official at Big City Transit today denied that potential fare increases are a deliberate attack on the poor. Transit spokesperson Tom Lee said that BCT couldn't guarantee there won't be huge fare gouging following a round of public relations exercises.

The proposed transit system reorganization is set to affect more than 22,000 transit workers, not to mention the 8,235,000 commuters who use the service daily.

There's been a lot of interesting talk about proposed changes in working hours and employee scheduling. We have to start by addressing the impact of any proposed new schedules or routes on transit users. How many of us might lose our transit service altogether under some hastily devised plan?

Transit riders have been led down the garden path before. Since 2002 there have been over a dozen studies, commissions and special investigations into public transit in the Big City area.

Thousands of trees have died so these reports can sit gathering dust somewhere. It looked like the new Board at BCT was on the right track, but their so-called 'expert' stepped right into the controversy.

"Tom Lee refuses to comment on secret plan"

In an exclusive Zonk interview, Tom Lee denied there was any secret plan to force "retired people and the poor" to hitchhike to get around.

In fact, Lee's exact words were "I have no comment on any secret plan."

When asked if he had any orders from the Mayor not to talk about fare increases, Mr. Lee said angrily "I don't report to the Mayor."

Rumours have circulated openly for some time now that strange shenanigans were afoot to bury the true costs of building fancy new Head Office digs. To date, cost overruns are expected to exceed twenty million dollars. That's our money. The Big City Boondoggle continues today folks.

This so-called public consultation is obviously nothing more than a smokescreen to cover corruption. Tom Lee's response was a big fat "No comment." And he's a consultation expert?

When asked if there's a hidden agenda to skyrocket fares to cover the new transit headquarters costs Lee insisted "No way is that true." Is this a plan to help special interests?

Today's Zonk goes out to Tom Lee, the cover-up artist at Big City Transit. If he knows anything about improving transit, he got off to a bad start today. If he's even aware of what's happening, he sure didn't show it in our meeting.

If you spot managerial incompetence anywhere, you know how to get hold of me. I'm Dennis Zonk.

Note to readers: Thanks for the best wishes, cards and notes on my 62nd birthday today.

Chapter 9

Tom Learns What "No Comment" Can Do

Three major mistakes in a media encounter:

Failing to understand the control relationships

Falling for negative and trap questions

Failing to structure and format your answers

Spin Defined

The instructor walked into the room and tossed the **Zonk** column on the table.

It was totally fictional, though Tom didn't know that yet. It was written during the time Tom had been listening to the lecture. It certainly looked real.

"Tom, here's a copy of the Dennis Zonk column that resulted from your little encounter. No one else will see it. Seems like we've got a lot of work to do here. Let's begin by reviewing the video of your interview."

"But when's the interview going to take place?" Tom asked.

"It already did. And as you can see, we've got a front-page story, with the potential for more coverage on the poverty issue. Plus future columns and possible sidebar stories on the headquarters scandal. In fact, this little encounter could produce several negative headlines."

Tom read the news column. He turned quite red. "How could this possibly happen? This headline is crazy. We didn't even start formally."

"Formally? You wrongly assumed there would be any formality. There was no expectation or agreement on formality here Tom. In order to formalize a relationship there have to be some basic ground rules established and understood on both sides.

"He didn't give you a chance to establish your role in this ambush encounter and you let him get away with it. We've now got your full attention, right? You were just interviewed and you've made the three most common mistakes in managing your message."

"What do you mean mistakes? What did I say that got me into so much trouble? We didn't even talk about scheduling, or the Mayor or the boondoggle. The fare issue is not important right now.

"Fares aren't even my responsibility really. This is just gross sensationalism and the lowest form of reporting. But then, that's what the media is like, right?"

"An ambush-style interview is a remote possibility that we have to prepare you for, Tom.

"Most reporters would have continued the interview to allow you to speak about your program, but even if the reporter had kept interviewing you, your earliest answers might still be the only ones used in the news story.

"The reporter could have chosen to edit everything else out later in the newsroom. This is an absolutely **extreme case of the reporter from hell**, but there are a few reporters out there who will use ambush techniques. You'll meet them soon enough."

"I just never thought it could happen to me so quickly," Tom said, his voice sounding rejected and fearful.

"You'll find that a very small percentage of reporters act like Dennis Zonk, and a small percentage of customers, too. Most reporters and customers are straightforward and decent people to work with, once you learn how they operate. Let's look at where you need immediate help.

"You made three **major** and very **simple** and very **common** mistakes.

"First, you failed to understand the reporter's control techniques. You let him steamroller you and take control of the interview.

"You needed to tell him and remind him what you were there to talk about. This establishes your role in the encounter.

"You need to learn how to properly set out the boundaries of your involvement in almost any communications encounter. You allowed Dennis Zonk to set the agenda here. It's a very common mistake among our new students."

"I did no such thing," Tom said weakly, and in complete denial.

"Every communications encounter, face to face or through the news media, has some form of **contract, consent or agreement,** no matter how formal or informal, stated or un-stated, written or un-written. The more you do it here in class, the more you'll learn the ropes. Think of it as a relationship in which each participant plays a role, whether it's a chosen role or one that's thrust upon you. In this situation, however, the reporter has pushed your limits and moved outside your role.

"You gave the reporter tacit consent to talk indirectly about a non-existent plan to make poor people hitchhike around the city. It was only a smokescreen, Tom. The reporter was throwing out this huge line and you went for his hook instead of delivering your message.

"It's sort of like a dance. You just let him lead. And sometimes that's the best way to dance, but not in this case.

"Secondly, see how you fell for Zonk's **negative questions**, trapping yourself into denials, defensiveness and argumentative, reactionary answers. You repeated or denied all his negative words."

"I did not," was Tom's immediate reaction, though he didn't say it out loud.

"We'll teach you to stop speaking in negatives and better manage the word **'not'**. He was able to put negative words in your mouth. *It's the most common reporter trap,* Tom. At least we think so. Every time you fell for the negatives in the questions, you got into trouble, like the political leader who once said *the president is not a moron.*

"You've been trapped into an argument by negative questioning and you gave the reporter reactive, negative and denial sound-bites on the most controversial topics."

"It's one of the easiest and sleaziest tricks reporters use to create controversy. Any personal encounter can turn into an argument, if you allow it. When emotion overcomes reason, wrong things can be said.

"The headlines and news story have already been written from this interview:"

Transit denies secret agenda to skyrocket fares

"Your issue, Tom, might suddenly become one of poor people hitchhiking. You've helped your critics position the issue negatively."

"That's impossible," Tom said. "I never said a thing to this guy, so how can he make me look so bad?"

"Tom, you replied indirectly about the Mayor, simply by using the word *Mayor* in an answer, so that a reporter could write: *'I don't report to the Mayor', the planner said angrily.*

"That's part of what's called journalistic licence Tom, although no one is ever sure exactly what journalistic license is at any given time. Another headline might read:

Big City Transit denies attack on the poor— can't rule out huge fare increase

"Or how about:

Transit refuses comment on secret fare-gouging plan

"Or maybe even:

Mayor not a moron, transit official says

"These are all examples of negative headlines. You helped create them. They result from the reactive, defensive messages in your answers. You didn't manage the negatives."

"How can they do that in the news media? I refused to talk about fares to this guy. He's way out of line if that's what the story says. We didn't even get started. I didn't even get his name."

"It's all part of negative questioning, Tom, and we've got a little training exercise to help you manage negativity. We call it the **Spin Doctor's Game**.

"Your third major mistake was failing to deliver your core messages in core structure. And in so doing, you missed all the opportunities to **go to message** and **stay on message**.

"You already had a message. Your briefing notes clearly stated *your job, your role* and *your work*. All you had to do was read from the material you used earlier today in the briefing session. Let's look at it from the top.

"You should have explained your job first, in order to keep the encounter in context. You need to get your role statement message out early and repeat it when you're in trouble.

"If you had stuck to your notes, you could have turned this interview around. All the answers you needed were in your briefing materials."

"He never gave me a chance," Tom replied.

"Tom, this shows what happens when you don't stick to your message. You went *off-message*. It could have hurt your career and your program, not to mention the future of public transit. This is a worst-case scenario, but we can help you prepare for this.

"We don't train many politicians here Tom, except for the rare ones we like. But even a politician can be trained to stick to the script. We have trained a lot of people who write scripts for politicians.

"Politicians learn early what can happen when they make it up as they go along. And corporate executives are much more in the news since the corporate scandals a decade ago led to greater reporting responsibilities. You're going to be out there with people watching you carefully.

"We'll teach you to write, edit, or build upon your own script, and then to stick to it. It's like building a bridge. You decide on the plan, you choose the building products and then you deliver the project.

"Let's review what you did using our 3-it diagram."

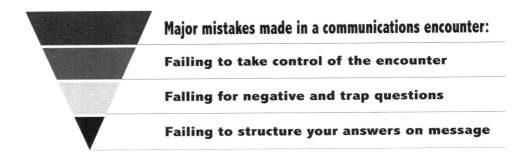

Major mistakes made in a communications encounter:

Failing to take control of the encounter

Falling for negative and trap questions

Failing to structure your answers on message

"We want to keep away from the politicians on this issue Tom, so let's not wave a red flag at them by even talking about them, mentioning them by name or by denying their involvement. If you get questions about them and the reporter is insistent, refer the reporter elsewhere.

"There are lots of techniques and we'll show you an expert using them.

"You'll learn to exhibit basic customer service skills in your messaging. Your message can show that you're aware of public concerns about the fare issue, that you're concerned about fares and that you're doing your share to move to the next steps which involve fares.

"If he talks about fares, remember this, Tom:

▶ First of all, you're working on routes and schedules.

▶ Routes and schedules are your first priority.

▶ Routes and schedules have to be handled first.

"You've got to become comfortable sounding like a broken record sometimes. It works.

"You've just reminded the reporter three times what you're there to talk about. These are each known as role-defining pillar statements that we talked about in the opening lecture."

"Can you help me?" Tom asked sheepishly.

"Of course. Pardon the old cliché but we're the experts and we're here to help. We love training engineers, lawyers and bureaucrats. They're always among the toughest people to train."

"But I don't really enjoy this stuff."

"Few people enjoy it Tom, not at first. They're afraid of failure, and that's a reasonable fear. Many people have a *fear of speaking in public,* and speaking through a reporter is one of the highest forms of public speaking.

"Some people have a fear of making mistakes or errors when controversial topics are raised, yet for the true public relations practitioner, a negative situation of any type is an opportunity to turn things around, as long as you're committed to making improvements.

"You can't do stupid things and expect to get positive news coverage. Doing good things doesn't assure you good news coverage, but it sure helps.

"When it comes to being a frontline spokesperson, it's not always about liking the work; it's about learning from the experts. It's about developing, defining and delivering your message, no matter what you're asked."

"You mean it's about **not answering a question**?"

"It's very much about answering questions, Tom. We're going to talk lots about nots.

"The secret is in answering negative questions in a way that **avoids the traps,** while reflecting on your commitment to serve the public. It's about using plain language and at the same time displaying your professionalism. Every horror question contains, somewhere deep inside, an opportunity question.

"It's about positioning yourself relating to others. Positioning yourself, your organization and your messaging as: Public-spirited, plain-talking and professional."

"You mean it's about **positive spin**? I'm not an opportunistic spin doctor," said Tom. "I'm a senior transit engineer."

"Ah hah! Your choice of words to describe yourself in that statement is an exercise in spin. You preferred the spin contained in the phrase **senior transit engineer** rather than the spin surrounding **opportunistic spin doctor**.

"I could say you were a glorified pavement jockey and that would be an example of spin on your job title. You wouldn't like that spin would you? Wouldn't you want to use your words to describe your job? Why would you choose to deny, and therefore repeat, negative words when you can use your own words? Spin doctors choose words that work for them."

Definition of Spin — SPIN College of Big City

Spin is the strategic choice of words, in an appropriate communications format, based on the right timing, place and messenger or method of delivery.

Or, formatted for SPIN College:

Spin is the strategic choice of words based on:

The timing of the delivery

The place of delivery

The medium, messenger or method of delivery

Chapter 10

Tom Makes Some Notes On Where He Went Wrong

During his break from class, Tom listed the following observations in his communicator.

The exact wording in the trap questions is tripping me up. Key words imbed themselves in my brain and I feel the overwhelming need to cleanse my mind and deny the question, by repeating the words because they're not true.

I keep denying the words or disagreeing with the content of the question. That creates my very first message. It is reactive, defensive and argumentative. Every brain cell is screaming out "No comment. No bloody comment."

It's like getting into a fight with a skunk, in this case, two skunks, an aggressive reporter and a headline-seeking politician. Could easily get on the first page, but wrong kind of publicity. Trouble is – the final audience will be my customers, who will see me embroiled in controversy. Got to remember the final recipient of message is not the reporter, but the reader or viewer.

My body language changes. Remembering that encounter with Zonk, I felt like I was a deer caught in headlights. I was like an out-of-touch professor, shocked that anyone would challenge me. My throat tightened up, pitch of voice changed, was holding my breath and forgetting to breathe. Clenched my fists, crossed my arms defensively, eyes were not sure where to look. Help.

I know it's emotion over reason. The questions triggered defensive emotions— fear, anger, even hostility. Then they combined with confusion, uncertainty, hurt feelings. It was like a slap in the face. I kept wondering why this question was being asked, what did I do to deserve this now?

Sure got off on wrong foot. Suddenly everything was slipping out of hand. The issues could suddenly take on a certain definition in the public's mind.

Can't really claim to be a victim. Few people know me, reputation is at stake; few are likely to jump to my aid at this stage. Why are they picking on me? Don't they see this is bullying?

Help.

Chapter 11

The Spin Doctor's Game

The Spin Doctor's Game:

Predicting negative words in horror questions

Re-defining the issue with YOUR words

The 3-it

Tips on avoiding:

Reactive statements

Defensive statements

Negative statements

As Tom looked at his personal communicator notes, he realized that everything on his list of observations was a **negative**.

In normal conversation we might be inclined to challenge others, get defensive or argumentative, but he realized Zonk had trapped him into using lots of dangerous little negative phrases in the interview.

Tom's mistake was in repeating the negatives by denying them, and the result had been extreme, but eye opening.

If the question was, *"Is the Mayor playing politics?"* or *"Is the Mayor a moron?"* it would be easy to answer, *"That's not true."*

Tom realized that if you replied to a reporter's question that way, the reporter could then easily quote you denying the horror words: **Official denies Mayor playing politics** or **Transit spokesperson says Mayor not a moron**.

You end up denying, *and adding* to someone else's spin.

Start by defining the issue in your own words. It would be better to say, *"The truth is that it's time to focus on the job of rebuilding transit in Big City."*

Lawyers, pay attention: In a court of law, a defence lawyer is required to **deny** a client is guilty. They must declare that they are not guilty even though the law is supposed to assume that they are *innocent*.

If you had to go to court, which of these three terms would you choose — *guilty, not guilty* or *innocent?*

When he got a horror question, the instructor told Tom to listen for the negative words without repeating, reacting or even referring to them.

"Your answers must *not* contain the word *not*."

Instead, he was to re-define the question, and then proceed to answer, using his definition of the issue.

There was a structured process to avoid the traps of the negativity. They had a name for this process at SPIN College.

It was officially called the **Reputation Vulnerability Assessment Analysis Model. (RVAAM)**

Some students called it *The Spin Doctor's Game*.

> *The Spin Doctor's Game* is designed to take control of the encounter, re-define the wording in the potential negative or trap questions and then add structure to the core message.

It was really everything they taught at SPIN College: Understanding control, avoiding negative traps and building structured core messages.

Here are some suggestions of how it starts — you'll add to these answers later.

Say there was a rambling, Zonk-like question thrown at you. Instead of using typical ways of answering, avoid the negative answer by changing the defining words.

SPIN College Tips on avoiding defensive / reactive / negative answers.

When you're asked negative questions:

Don't say:	Instead Say:
No comment.	*I'm sorry, can I get back to you later? I don't know the answer to that question.* Or, *You should really speak to…*
We haven't failed.	*We ran into some real problems.*
Don't blame us for this mess.	*We're sorry for any inconvenience. We're working with the blank agency, whose job it is to repair the water damage.*
It wasn't all that bad.	*This was a serious situation for this group, this group and ourselves. That's why we're working to do this, this and this.*
We're not ignoring anyone.	*We realize that there are some people who are still not satisfied. We ask them to keep in mind concerns like this, this and this.*
That's not really important.	*What's really important right now is this. Let's look at this, this and this.*
That's not really the issue.	*That issue is important. What's also important is…*

That's not my department.	*I work in the (blank) department. I'd be pleased to answer any questions you have about this department.*
I can't help you with that.	*I can help you with this.*
Accidents can happen.	*Safety is our number one priority.*
It's not our fault.	*We're anxious to find out what happened.*
We didn't do it.	*This situation resulted from this, this and this.*
I can't guarantee.	*We're working to improve this. I can guarantee that there's a plan in place to deal with the issue of…*
I can't speculate.	*Let's wait and see, shall we? Or: I don't know yet. Ask me that question after the trial/investigation/clean-up. Right now we're focussing on this, this and this.*
I really can't talk to you now.	*I'd be glad to talk to you just as soon as…*
I can't talk about him/her.	*The Privacy Act prohibits me from releasing that information.*
No comment.	*I'd be happy to answer questions about…*

Tom had gotten into real trouble because almost all of Zonk's questions had been about the Mayor, the new board, and the scandals around the headquarters' costs. Zonk had tried to create an expectation that it was Tom who could solve every transit problem. He had to remind folks of his share of the task at hand — the survey.

He realized that when he was asked off-topic questions, he could use them as an opportunity to talk about his responsibility — making sure everyone completed the survey.

When he was asked about being a cover-up artist, Tom learned to say how everyone would be surveyed, when they would be surveyed or where they would be surveyed — no cover up there.

All these negatives reminded Tom of one of his Aunt Betty's stories, although her version usually included more colourful language.

The Story of the Negative Family

Once upon a time there was a family called the Negatives, Ned and Nellie Negative. They worked for THE GOVERNMENT.

Ned's favourite expression was, "We can't do that. It won't work. We've never done it that way before."

Nellie liked to say, "It's not my department. I can't help you. I have no idea."

Naturally, with two negative genes, their child, Pollyanna was born a positive child. She had a discouragingly positive approach to life, her parents thought.

Ned and Nellie wanted to turn the child away from her positive outlook, so on her 12th birthday, her parents presented her with a manure pile.

Pollyanna became so excited. Grinning ear to ear, she dashed toward the pile. To her parents' bewilderment, she grew increasingly happy and more excited.

Perplexed, Ned asked, "Why are you so happy with getting a pile of horse manure for your birthday? You should be feeling depressed like us."

"Gosh Dad," she replied, "with all this horse manure, I just know there's a pony in there somewhere!"

Managing the negatives is often about finding the pony in a manure pile. Tom had to find some way of looking at negative questions as opportunities.

In 1999, SPIN College's founder developed a list of about 400 negative, inflammatory words and phrases that, in certain contexts, could be used to develop negative questions.

The original list is contained in his book, *MediaSpeak*. An updated list appears in the appendix to this book. Feel free to add some of your own to the list.

A negative question might begin with: "Why have you failed to…"

Who says you've failed? Why might people think you're failing? Is it even true?

The spin doctor's challenge is to replace the word "failed." Maybe you're still working on that issue.

The secret is NOT to **deny** or **repeat** the word "failed" in your answer, or the headline will read *Transit denies failure*.

It would be wrong to deny failure, since then all of the story's spin might centre on failure. Your goal is to *change the spin* away from any *failure*.

The challenge is to replace the word "failed" without denying or repeating it, because the question is not necessarily true – it contains a false premise. If you're still working on an issue, chances are you haven't **failed**.

Was there a failure to address the issue of transit rates in Tom's program? The reporter, customer or politician may have asked something like, "Why does this plan fail to address the public's concerns about sky-rocketing transit fares?"

When this happens, your mind often focuses on the negative word *failure* and something inside you screams out to deny it, to refute or to repeat the word failure. The question is based on a highly arguable, perhaps even false premise. All of the spin will be around the word "failure".

Even if you were to answer with "That's not the case." or even "No." the reporter can still quote you *indirectly*.

The result could be stated: "Mr. Lee **denied that** Big Transit **had failed** to address concerns about skyrocketing fares.

In this case, you would have refuted the negative, but you still reacted to the question and referred to the negatives indirectly. The reporter can now quote you, even if it's done indirectly. It happens a lot in the news, except to students of SPIN College.

The challenge is to figure out what the question is really about. Where's the pony in the question, the opportunity to deliver your message?

Tom thought of the **Spin Doctor's Game** as good word/bad word. It allowed him to avoid the traps of negative questioning, and served as a constant reminder to stay on-message. It allowed him to avoid controversy.

When you are asked why you've failed to do something, you're really being asked about what it is that **you *are* doing, *have done* or *are working on doing*.** These are your 'ponies'.

It's not always about finding the opposite to failure. Chances are you already have a core statement that describes what it is that you (and your team) are doing. So use it.

The Spin Doctor's Game required Tom to come up with simple, short words to **disprove negative stereotypes** or to disprove the **false premise** in the question about failure.

As an exercise, Tom was asked to list words or phrases to describe bureaucrats that had negative connotations. One of the first words that Tom thought of was **lazy**.

Variations were: *under worked, overpaid, out of touch, paper-pusher,* even just the word *bureaucrat* can evoke *insensitive, uncaring, narrow minded* in some people's minds.

> ▷ **Tip:** The best way to overcome the perception of being lazy is to use the word *"work."* It's a great little word that can seldom be over-used.

▶ "We're working to improve transit.

▶ We're working to help transit users...

▶ We're working with groups like...

▶ We're working on a plan that will..."

The SPIN College Negative Question Model:

Take a question with a negative word or phrase, then create an answer, and replace the negative with a word or pillar point of your choosing.

Instead of denying failure, you talk about your work, your role, your goals.

Then, 3-it. Build on it by adding three support messages and sparklers.

Example:

Reporter From Hell: "Is your failure to prevent contract cost overruns on the Headquarters boondoggle due to mismanagement or incompetence? And, do you accept personal responsibility for this fiasco?"

The Reporter From Hell calls this the mind-blower question. When you're asked if you accept personal responsibility, your brain can get strangled or side-tracked easily. It's a cheap trick some questioners use.

What is the question really about? How can it be about what you want it to be about?

Where's the pony in the question?

How does your core statement or message relate to this question?

At its core, the question is about contract administration. That's all.

You want to show:

▶ you're aware of what's happening in construction contract administration,

▶ that you care about its impact, and

▶ that you are doing your share to make improvements.

You then volunteer some strategic detail to serve as an example of what you're doing.

Answer: "Let me tell you about some of the improvements we're making in our contract administration." (This is called a bridging support statement)

"Improving contract administration is a big priority for Big City Transit's construction office."

(This is called a defining, or <u>what</u> pillar — defining your concern, stating <u>what</u> you're concerned about, followed by three <u>how</u> pillars to show <u>how</u> you're dealing with this concern.)

▶ "That's why we've introduced a new tendering system. **(1)**
▶ "That's why we have new contract monitoring in place. **(2)**
▶ "That's why we're investigating the work being done at the new headquarters project. **(3-it)**

"One of the features of the new tendering system is a requirement that all contractors post a bond…"

(This is a <u>for instance</u> that might go on for several minutes, depending on the spokesperson's subject knowledge.)

RFH: "Why are you dragging your feet on this decision to build a new bus station? Is this due to political pressure from the Mayor's office, or are you purposely creating a crisis?"

Are you really dragging your feet? What is the question about? *Where's the pony?*

It's about the planning, scheduling and decision-making process.

At its core, the question is about *when you're doing it* and *what are the reasons for its present schedule.* **It's a question about the process**.

The issue must be **redefined** from *dragging your feet.* You need to explain the changes that have been made in the process, and why. Re-define the issue, 3-it and build on the 3-it.

 Answer: "Let me bring you up to date on the changes we've made to our planning schedule and why we've made them."

(Bridge directly to your <u>what</u> pillar in the first, opening sentence, then add a framing pillar point — <u>why</u> we've made changes.)

"We've changed this…we've changed this…and we've changed this. (3-it)

Or,

*"The most important things being done are (this, this and this).
Once we complete that work, a decision will be made on the construction start date, the completion date and the opening date."*

Or,

*"The most important things that will happen next are (this, this and this).
Let me tell you about a special new feature called…" (a for instance or example).*

▷ **Tip:** Framing pillars frame or position an issue, and can take the form of a question.

Example: If you want to make the issue one of trust, you might say: "The issue facing voters is, who can they trust?"

RFH Getting Warmed Up Question(s): "Why have you **ignored the concerns** of senior citizens and people on fixed incomes and pensions? If rates skyrocket, will they be able to afford to take transit anymore? Have you no concern for the poor, sir? How much do you expect they'll suffer as a result?"

What is the question (several questions actually) about?

It's about people's concerns. Do you care about people?

Ignoring? — that's a false premise again, but if you say you're *not ignoring* them, people may wonder why you're being so defensive.

Redefine the issue in the question, 3-it and build on it. This question, at its core, is about what you're doing and how it will affect certain publics. That's the easiest pony to find — helping the public.

Answer: "The goal of this program is to improve transit for everyone, including riders who don't use transit to get to work." (Role-defining pillar statement – a big-tent pillar that tells people your main job is to help everyone)

"That's why we're working with groups like the Big City Seniors Council, the Big City Tenants Society and the Association of Retired Persons.

"Let me tell you about a meeting we held last week with the…"

(This example shows you are in touch with the issue because you are practising MBWA — management by walking around)

RFH Still At It Question: "Why have you **failed to address** the fares issue? Are you under orders from the Mayor to **create a stunt** to divert attention from the headquarters **boondoggle**?"

Answer: "Big Transit will be **working on the fare issue** in stage three of our renewal plan." (Pillar statement that says, in effect, fares are someone else's department.)

"Our **first priority** is to deal with routes and schedules. **Next**, the team responsible for equipment will focus on those needs, and **then** the fares assessment team will examine fares.

"**I'd be pleased to give you the contact numbers for the heads of those teams.** (referral)

"In the first phase…"

RFH Who Won't Give Up Question: "Why are you **abandoning** the political process by conducting public consultations directly with users? Have you **abdicated your responsibility** to our duly elected officials?"

(*"Abandon"* is the first *"Opportunity Word"* in the list from **The Spin Doctor's Game** in the appendix of this book. *"Abdicated"* is next on the list.)

Answer: "Big City Transit is committed to public consultation. This plan was approved by the Big City Board of Consumers. Transit users will have direct involvement in the future of their system.

"We're **changing** the way we do transit planning. We've introduced new … we've … and we've also …

"For example, our new information centre can handle… "

Now you've used the word *change* to re-define this issue. Change is not always popular, but few can deny it's happening. It's a good common sense word and often inarguable.

> ▷ **Tip:** Anytime there's a *not* in your message, chances are it can be replaced. It's almost always better to say what you are doing than to say what you're *not* — unless the *nots* are purposeful and planned.

Consider how these denial answers would have sounded as quotable quotes:

*We have **not** failed to …*

*We're **not** dragging our feet on …*

*We're **not** ignoring the needs of seniors on …*

*We're **not** abandoning …*

Part of the challenge is to understand the communications format in which negative messaging can thrive. It is at its most damaging during a media encounter that will be subject to later editing — and that's most media encounters.

There are a few exceptions to the use of the word NOT.

It's fine to use a negative word or phrase when it's purposeful, planned or used to inflame an issue. The dangers lurk when the negative word is unexpected and you react by repeating it.

We'll never stop using negative language; we just need to understand the danger of the resulting answer.

Tom would forever remember the Spin Doctor's Game:

▶ Predict a possible horror question or negative wording.
▶ Avoid negative reaction by re-defining the question.
▶ Reply with a structured core message.

Tom was about to see an expert handle Zonk.

Chapter 12

Tanya's Interview

An expert takes control as:

Public-spirited

Plain-talking

Professional

Tom and the instructor moved into the studio to watch a videodisc. It was a simulated interview between *"Dennis Zonk"* and a woman identified as Tanya Merkle.

Tanya was a former student at SPIN College, now working as Vice President of Big City Energy Services. During her time as a student, she was coached by George Olds, SPIN College's chief training designer.

She did extremely well, and became the model for SPIN College's computer-simulated cyber spokesperson, or CSP.

She liked the acronym; it was the same as the one she held as a Certified Speaking Professional in Big City's Association of Professional Speakers (BCAPS).

Once she had been provided with messages, she could handle any encounter. The CSP program had already been tested on TV newscasts and no one had noticed, but it was still top-secret.

SPIN College figured if the news media could create cyber-newscasters, surely there was a need for cyber-spokespersons.

Tom had no idea he was watching a CSP being interviewed by Dennis Zonk on the video — a re-creation of what Tom had just been through, with Tanya playing his role. Her memory bank had been programmed with a copy of Tom's speech notes and background materials.

He looked forward to seeing how she would fare, since she obviously would know little about transit planning or engineering matters. Tom figured the columnist would make mincemeat out of her in no time.

Tom watched Tanya walk confidently into the room and over to the reporter/columnist. She extended her hand and introduced herself. She was even smiling, he noted. That probably won't last long with this old reporter, Tom thought.

Tanya: "Good morning, I'm Tanya Merkle. You must be Dennis Zonk. I've been following your columns on the transit improvement plan. I'm pleased to have a chance to meet you and talk specifically about the public consultation survey for routes and scheduling. This is going to be a big program.

"Why don't we grab a reconstituted, simulated, coffee-type beverage product and go sit by the window over there," she continued, smiling as ever.

Zonk: "So I hear you've got some secret plan to bring in major fare increases," Dennis Zonk barked at Tanya as they sat down. He was just as gruff as he had been with Tom.

Tanya paused for just a moment, and Tom thought she might melt.

Instead, she took a deep breath, smiled and seemed to count silently to three before she spoke.

Tanya: (enthusiastically) "Let me tell you about our public consultation plans that will lead up to discussions on fares."

Smooth, Tom thought. She was so perky; she was almost starting to get on his nerves.

Zonk continued to grill Tanya.

Zonk: "What will a fare increase do to retired people and the poor – are you going to make them hitchhike to get around?"

Tom's mouth dropped open as Tanya repeated the very first line from his speech.

Tanya: "We're here today to start consultation on a new transit system that will serve workers, businesses and consumers…"

Tom watched as Zonk broke into the middle of one of Tanya's answers. He was very good when it came to rude.

Zonk: "Come on, everyone knows this so-called public consultation of yours is nothing more than a clever smokescreen to hide the political damage created by the Mayor's old pals on the transit board. Have you got any orders from the Mayor not to talk about this?"

Tanya: "The main purpose of the consultation program is to hold information meetings, to encourage people to complete their transit surveys, and to report our results along with the technical data."

Zonk: "Ms. Merkle, do you deny that there's a hidden agenda to skyrocket fares to cover the new transit headquarters cost overruns?"

Tanya: "Fares are the final stage of the consultation. First, we have to work on some recommendations about routes and schedules. Next, we'll look at a wide range of equipment needs. Then, we'll be able to discuss fares."

Zonk still went for the jugular.

Zonk: "Oh come on, there are thousands of retired people out there who want to know whether they'll be able to afford to take transit in the future or whether they'll be forced to stay in their homes. And what about the disabled? And the poor? They feel they either can't use or can't afford to use the system. Why have you ignored THEIR needs?" He was almost salivating at the mouth.

Tanya (very calmly and very firmly): "Big City Transit is working to meet the needs of all potential riders. Since the turn of the century there have been major demographic changes in Big City. Retired people make up a large part of our present ridership — they're loyal, they tend to ride at off-peak hours, and they use the service almost exclusively.

"Fully 32% of the population is over 65.

"Another 24% of the baby-boomers will reach that age within five years.

"There are 25% more people with mobility challenges than just five years ago.

"And 26% of families are now living below the poverty line, according to the Big City Statistics Bureau's latest report.

"These people know their needs; our job is to find out more about those needs.

"We're looking forward to having them take part in the surveys because this is about re-building public transit to serve riders like them.

"New transit routes and new schedules are to be brought in within a year; that's what we're starting to do today."

Zonk: (grinning madly and trying again) "So, what do you think motivates the Mayor here? Do you suppose she's in political trouble over the transit headquarters boondoggle?"

Tanya: "I'm best able to answer questions about what is motivating this project. That's really my area of expertise."

Zonk: "Is this an attempt on the part of the Mayor at headline grabbing at your expense? In your opinion, Ms Merkle, is the Mayor a moron for taking this position?"

Tanya: "It was my understanding that this interview was about our public consultation survey, and I'd be pleased to answer your questions about that."

And with that, Tanya moved right back into the main part of her message. She had "moved to message" about how consultation would take place. Then she kept talking and stayed "on message" — **her** message.

Tanya: "Our automated transit survey downloads the information as passengers enter their travels plans. Users simply outline their origin and destination points on a map on the screen and the computer enters the information into the survey database.

"Or they can enter their needs with a voice-activated program that allows them to answer the questions with their personal communicator.

"It's really fun. Come on over here and I'll show you how it works. Where might you be using transit, Mr. Zonk? We can map it out right now if you like."

Zonk: "You can call me Ian- er, Dennis. Show me how to get to the Big City Bugle offices from the west side."

And with that, Tanya had Zonk's undivided attention. The reporter's inquisition had turned into a fact-filled briefing by Tanya. It lasted about 30 minutes.

Finally, he thanked her, gathered his things and left.

"He actually thanked her," Tom thought.

"Not bad for a robot, eh Tom?" The instructor said, and then explained about the CSP.

"He thanked a robotic, simulated cyber-spokesperson. What was this world coming to?" said Tom, utterly confused. "Could you explain how she, er, 'it' managed to get on Zonk's side for me? She certainly had a different outcome, and I want to know her secrets."

Chapter 13

SPIN College Tools

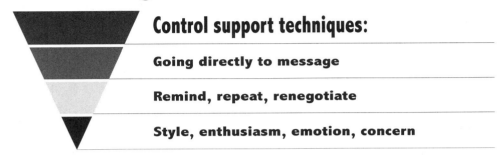

Control support techniques:

Going directly to message

Remind, repeat, renegotiate

Style, enthusiasm, emotion, concern

Support statements and phrases:

Bridges, baits and re-asks

Techniques to handle questions

Delivering your message

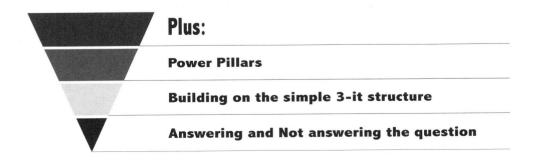

Plus:

Power Pillars

Building on the simple 3-it structure

Answering and Not answering the question

"Let's review that videodisc again, this time with the instructional popups activated — and examine what Tanya did differently," said the instructor.

"First of all, notice how Tanya walked confidently into the room and over to the reporter/columnist. She extended her hand and introduced herself. She was even smiling," he noted.

"Her whole attitude is positive, confident and assured. She began by taking the active lead in the encounter."

Tanya: "Good morning, I'm Tanya Merkle. You must be Dennis Zonk. I've been following your columns on the transit improvement plan. I'm pleased to have a chance to meet you and **talk specifically about the consultation process for routes and scheduling**. This is going to be a big survey program."

"Tom, notice that in a very few words, she had, in effect made a short, succinct and polite offer to the reporter — a **contract**, in effect — and having heard no disagreement, she could now fulfill her part of the offer."

Tom wondered why he hadn't had the politeness and manners to introduce himself as Tanya had done. She had a certain class, he thought. Was she real or what, he wondered. He'd heard about some of SPIN College's experiments.

This time, a popup on the videodisc explained how Tanya had just taken control of the encounter. Tanya took control in a very polite way.

She **had set the limits of her participation** on what she intended to talk about in this brief encounter – she was glad to talk about the consultation process for routes and schedules.

By implication, she would **confine her messages to that topic**. She had not agreed to talk about anything else. Anything else was open to renegotiation.

Tanya had been able to stick to her message, in part, because she had **contracted** her role.

When Tanya said she'd been following Dennis Zonk's columns, she served notice that she was **aware** of Zonk's take on the issues. She knew what format his columns appeared in, and his probable approach to this issue, so she got down to business quickly.

Tanya: "Why don't we grab a reconstituted, simulated, coffee-type beverage product and go sit by the window over there," Tanya continued, smiling as ever.

Zonk: "So I hear you've got some secret plan to bring in major fare increases." Zonk ignored her **contract**.

Tanya paused for just a moment, took a deep breath, smiled and seemed to count silently to three before she spoke.

Tanya: (enthusiastically) "Let me tell you about our public consultation plans that will lead to discussions on fares."

With that one simple sentence, a popup explained, Tanya had expertly demonstrated 3 of SPIN College's support tools — bridging, reinforcing, and enthusiastic delivery.

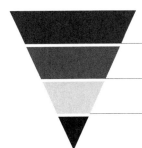

Support tools for interviews:

Support phrases such as bridges, baits, re-asks

Techniques such as reminding, re-negotiating and repetition

Delivering your message

Definitions:

Support phrases are little aids to help you manage the interaction with reporters (and customers, for that matter). They are used to separate the question from the answer, or to re-define the issue.

Bridges are connector phrases, like:

"Let me explain what's happening."

"Let's look at the facts."

"Let me bring you up to date on the situation."

A bridge moves you to message.

1. Bridging to, or going directly to a planned message is the **number one control technique** in media encounters.

Tanya had not only bridged to her message – "Let me tell you about our public consultation plans" – she'd done it **enthusiastically** and **politely**, without defensiveness.

When you say, "Let me explain what we're doing…" or "Let me bring you up to date on what's happening here…," what is the reporter going to say — no? You've just given the reporter a signal that you've got a self-contained package of information and that you've thought about it ahead of time. Now, follow through with interesting, concise and factual information and you're a winner.

Whenever controversy arose, Tanya would politely say something like, "Let me explain what we're doing." Clearly the bridging tactic worked. The reporter let her explain.

There were many **defining phrases** programmed into the CSP for when a reporter went off topic, such as...

The real issue here is…

Our main concern is…

What we're really talking about is…

This is really about…

The main job right now is to…(role defining reminder)

Let's get back on track, shall we?

Let's be very clear about what's happening here.

Bait — You can bait a reporter in a live encounter through the mere mention of a tantalizing topic, without any elaboration. Then stop speaking. Create a pause or when the interview is live, create dead air. Then wait.

This forces the reporter to ask a follow-up question on that topic. It works best in live encounters, and if baiting doesn't work the first time, try again.

Example of a baiting technique in an interview:

Question: "Do you really expect transit riders to participate in this survey?"

Answer: "Many riders want their opinions heard when it comes to improving the system. And, of course there are the big prizes to be won." (Baiting statement)

Question: "Oh, what kind of prizes?" (Hooked)

Answer: "We're offering custom leather bomber jackets to the first 1,000 people who complete the survey."

Question: "Won't that crash the computer?"

Answer: "In our surveys in the Big Cities formerly known as Los Angeles, London and Tokyo, we were able to handle…"

Re-asks — questions you ask a reporter in the middle of an interview, sometimes to buy yourself time to develop your answer, sometimes to clarify the question, and sometimes to send a *slow down* signal to the reporter.

Some SPIN College favourites:

Could you please repeat the first part of your question?

I'm not sure I understand what you're asking me.

Can you be a bit more specific?

Could you re-phrase that question please? (What would a reporter say — no?)

Tanya **reminded** the reporter of what they had verbally contracted to talk about — and by implication what she would not talk about. She had, in effect, **reinforced the negotiation** of her involvement in the interview mid-stream.

---

2. Reminding the reporter of your role or core message through reinforcing, renegotiation and repetition, is the **second major control technique**.

Repetition is one of most important control devices, even if you end up sounding like a broken record. When used effectively, you're making it clear to the reporter that you are being repetitive on purpose.

Repetition puts the reporter on notice that you intend to say specific things in specific ways – again and again, if necessary. It's essential if the reporter is being repetitive. If a reporter keeps repeating questions on controversial topics, you have to repeat your message too. Repetition fails without content.

Repetition does not guarantee you'll be quoted saying something, but it sure helps.

▷ **Tip:** Avoid phrases like "As I said before…", "Like I said earlier…"or "Once again, I'd like to stress…" They're wasted words since they won't make sense if heard out of context, and would likely be edited out of any print or TV news item.

3. **Delivery methods** — the use of pauses, speaking style, politeness — is the **third important control technique**.

Tanya had a style of delivery that couldn't be taught; it could only be built upon.

Before she even replied to Zonk's insinuations, Tanya paused, took a breath and seemed to count to three.

It gave her time to collect her thoughts and think of what she wanted to say next. And she kept smiling. Appearing comfortable and in full control, she was able to use her core messages to stickhandle around his horror questions.

The **use of silence** (or the **purposeful pause**) sends out strong signals that aren't likely to get you into much trouble.

Reporters sometimes pause to get the interviewee to speak more, reveal more, admit more. When faced with a hostile customer, saying nothing is often the best practise, or at least the most tactful at that moment.

Tanya maintained a pleasant attitude at all times. Her **speaking style** supported her core messages; she was friendly and always spoke **enthusiastically.**

If you've got a smile in your voice, it helps you position yourself as **personable, polite** and **approachable**.

When you've got a smile on your face, you appear relaxed and confident.

Broadcast encounters call for a certain level of perkiness and enthusiasm, unless it's a sad situation, a tragedy or a serious loss for someone.

> Tom's Aunt Betty used to say, "Always be polite, whether you like it or not."

Meanwhile, back on the videodisc, Dennis Zonk continued to grill Tanya as roughly as he had done with Tom. What was different was how she handled it.

Zonk: "What will a fare increase do to retired people and the poor – are you going to make them hitchhike to get around?"

Tanya: "We're here today to start consultation on a new transit system that will serve workers, businesses and consumers."

The training disc explained that Tanya had used a **Power Pillar** — a strong point or statement that defines the issue, followed by a supporting **3-it** to describe three elements pertaining to the statement.

> **Definition — Power Pillars**
> A Power Pillar contains four elements — a defining premise point or statement, followed by three stand-alone points or statements (a 3-it) to prove or support the premise.

Here's a favourite Power Pillar Template:

Our main concern is improving (public transit).

> ▶ **That's why we're building...**

> ▶ **That's why we're working...**

> ▶ **That's why we're helping...**

A variation:

We're working to improve transit.

> ▶ **We've got a plan to address routes, schedules and fares.**

> ▶ **We're working with groups like workers, businesses, and consumers.**

> ▶ **We're starting with school groups, then seniors, and finally we'll be asking employers for their help.**

> *Power Pillars are often picked up as sound-bites, because they're short, sweet and to the point.*
>
> ▷ **Tip:** Speak the above sentence out loud and you will hear a decent sound-bite. It comes in under 7 seconds, and contains a premise point, supported with a cliché in the form of a 3-it that explains the premise.

3-it

Our lives are filled with threes: 3 guys walk into a bar, 3 easy payments, 3 times a lady. They're easy on the speaker, the listener and the reporter.

A 3-it contains 3 examples, parts or elements that support your main pillar point. For instance, the points could describe the work, the team and the plan, or talk about the past, the present, and the future.

Each of these parts can be further broken down or explained in threes, depending on the length and detail the encounter needs.

Example:

▶ People will benefit from this program, especially customers, employees and special needs riders.

You could then go on in your message to identify three types of customer, three types of employee and three types of special needs riders who will benefit.

Then find three benefits for each of those types (there are at least 9 now):

▶ Safer, faster and cheaper. Or, Better X, improved Y, and lower Z.

You can develop a 3-it by anticipating simple, easy questions that may arise around your issue.

In the example above, we started by asking ourselves, *Who will benefit? How will they benefit? When...*

Then you can play mix and match with various 3-it combinations for **Power Pillars, briefings or speeches**:

▶ 3 steps
▶ 3 contributing factors
▶ 3 results

▶ 3 concerns
▶ 3 goals
▶ 3 actions necessary to achieve them

- 3 important statistics
- 3 components
- 3 requirements

- 3 statements that show you're aware
- 3 things you're doing that show you care
- 3 ways others can do their share

Other examples:

What are the steps in an investigation, or how do you manage a crisis?

- Assess the situation
- Determine priorities
- Assign resources

What are you doing?

We're doing this in the following ways: (list 3 of them). We're doing this in steps (list the 3 steps). And we're doing this with our partners _____, _____ and _____. (name the 3 partners)

Why are you doing it?

- The main reasons are…(list 3 reasons)

What caused this situation?

- There were several contributing factors, including _____, _____ and _____.

Tom was an engineer and the 3-it was easy for him to remember, easy to use and easy to adapt. He appreciated the pervading focus on three's. When learning anything, you had to start with a basic structure. Later on you adapted the structure to your own style

The 3-it was a tool for the spoken word as well as the written word. Reporters loved them, as did most audiences. They're easy for the speaker to use, easy for a reporter to remember, and easy on the listener or reader, too.

> ▷ **Tip:** Avoid saying the word "three" when you deliver your 3-it message. It draws attention to the structure of your answer and away from the content of your answer.

Expanding the 3-it with sparklers

Definition — Sparkler

A sparkler is a case study, example or for instance. It serves as a **proof statement** to your pillar points. Sparklers give you credibility, display your subject knowledge and create visualizations for the message recipient. They can run for a couple of seconds or for several minutes in your required message format.

Sparklers can serve as **stand-alone answers** in an interview — they show that you're there to talk. They work best when they're volunteered. Don't wait to be asked.

It's often not enough to say you care about safety on the road. You may not have the credibility to be believed. You may need to add a sparkler, such as, "Let me give you an example of some of the concrete repair work we're doing on the bridge deck..."

Sparklers provide proof after a pillar. (Pillar:) "We're re-building public transit. (Sparkler:) This study into routes and schedules, for instance, will take six months of research, meetings and rider input. We've opened our main information centre at Central Station. The centre will be open from..."

There are naturally three main types of sparklers:

▶ Stand-alone for instances, summaries or briefings like: "Just last week we saw the first results of..." or "Let's look at the history of..." or "Let me bring you up to date on our investigation."

▶ A literary visualization — bringing something to life with words, so that the message recipient can visualize the situation in an easy way: "For the average consumer it means that..."

▶ Maps, visual aids, photo opportunities, diagrams, graphs, stunts, special effects, staging, charts, signage, simulated models and other visuals can also act as sparklers to your message: "That will affect homes in the area south west of the zoo here on this Big City map."

Tom started to see more opportunities for 3-its in longer messages:

It's an all-new planning system that will:

    ▶ **examine over 20 potential locations for new transit hubs. (Let me give you some examples of locations where...)**

    ▶ **bring together seven existing transit systems, for instance in Westhaven...**

    ▶ **result in an energy-efficient, customer-oriented system serving all of Big City. The new wind turbines, for example, will mean...**

The main message has now gone from sound-bite to **power briefing**, by merely add sparkling content to the 3-it.

Each of the individual sparklers increases the content, length and believability of your message.

Tom continued to watch the video, as Zonk broke into the middle of one of Tanya's answers. "Yes, he was very good at rude," Tom reconfirmed his first impression.

Zonk: "Come on, everyone knows this so-called public consultation of yours is nothing more than a clever smokescreen to hide the political damage created by the Mayor's old pals on the transit board. Have you got any orders from the Mayor not to talk about this?"

Tanya: "The main purpose of the consultation program is to hold information meetings, to encourage people to complete their transit surveys, and to report our results along with the technical data."

Tom recognized the use of a 3-it just as the pop-up appeared.

Zonk: "Do you deny that there's a hidden agenda to skyrocket fares to cover the new transit headquarters cost overruns?"

Tanya could have denied the reporter's conjecture. She could have become caught up in the emotions that fare increases could bring. She could have started an argument or gotten huffy. She could have fallen for dangerous speculation.

Instead, she stayed **on message**.

Tanya: "Fares are the final stage of the consultation. First, we have to work on some recommendations about routes and schedules. Next, we'll look at a wide range of equipment needs. Then, we'll be able to discuss fares."

A *Power Pillar,* thought Tom — even before the pop-up confirmed his thoughts. A strong statement, supported by three parts. It was concise, fact-filled and strategic. Maybe he was catching on after all.

This Tanya was a firecracker, Tom thought. She was beginning to make him excited at the prospect of the work ahead of him.

Tanya didn't even seem to acknowledge Zonk's horror questions. She refused to go for the bait. Instead, she found opportunities to go to her message. She avoided the negative traps in the questions and instead delivered her message with enthusiasm and with strong, fact-filled answers. She kept smiling. Her answers weren't even original; they were lifted from Tom's speech notes.

Tanya had found the ponies in the horror questions.

And her answers were certainly better than "No comment."

She came across as public spirited, plain talking and professional. Her content won over controversy.

Tom had seen politicians who refused to answer questions, often because of their own special agenda, yet he knew that he had an agenda too. It amounted to doing his job: becoming **aware** of transit needs, showing that he **cared** about good transit, and doing his **share** to improve transit.

It's NOT the Questions. It's the Answers.

"What about those politicians you see who never answer the questions directly?" Tom asked his instructor.

"Tom, it's all about directness — how directly or indirectly one was ready, willing or able to answer a question. There are three contributing factors, of course."

1. Format

The instructor explained that the viewer's reaction to someone **going to message** instead of **not answering the question** depended first of all on the format of the interview.

"If the interview was live, Tom, or if the reporter's question was repeated in the news story, the resulting answer might look manipulative following the original question. Usually the question is edited out – most media interviews are subject to later editing, and a story will end up using only a small portion of a self-contained answer such as a five word quote or a six second sound-bite.

"If you develop answers that stand alone, without the question having to be repeated, the question can become irrelevant, or at least unnecessary."

The Spin Doctor's Game is designed to make questions unnecessary. Use a technique like a bridge, and move directly and smoothly to the main message.

A pause can also help move the answer away from the question; and nobody paused like Tanya, Tom noticed. She used repetition effectively too.

2. Content

Not answering the question depended upon having a good answer ready, especially if it was content-rich and delivered in plain talk enthusiastically, or with the proper emotion.

It looks bad when a politician says nothing of any real substance, lacks enthusiasm or couches phrases in bureaucratic jargon. If you can't answer part of a question, you should answer another part substantively, or at least make it process-oriented.

In other words, you might not be able to talk about how a political decision was made, but you might be able to talk about how the program would unfold within your office or division. **Stake out your share of the issue and talk about your share**.

The way you got the listener/viewer/reader/customer onside was to make yourself (or your work) interesting, informative and relevant to the main issue.

When you say, "The main thing here is safety," you've just made the issue really relevant to almost everyone.

Safety is an *inarguable premise,* just as if you'd said, "We're working to improve customer service." Of course, you'll have to prove it by stating 3 things you're doing to improve it, with some examples or sparklers.

3. The viewer, listener, reader's pre-existing opinions

How someone is perceived answering a question depends on the viewer's pre-disposition to the person being interviewed. Recipients of the message will filter it through their own biases, knowledge, opinions and experiences. They'll come to conclusions about you very quickly.

A perfect example is the Big City Mayor.

If you dislike her and she's not answering the question, then you'll look negatively at the encounter. It confirms your suspicions that she's manipulative, overbearing and hiding something.

If you support her, then you'll think she really succeeds in putting the reporter in her/his place.

If you're undecided, the result will depend on her content and delivery — or on how well the ideas are sold because of her enthusiasm, style and presentation skills.

Tanya's training video continued with 'Dennis Zonk' still trying for the jugular.

Zonk: "Oh come on. There are thousands of retired people out there who want to know whether they'll be able to afford to take transit in the future or whether they'll be forced to stay in their homes. And what about the disabled?

And the poor? They feel they either can't use or can't afford to use the system. Why have you ignored THEIR needs?"

Tanya: "Big City Transit is working to meet the needs of all potential riders. Since the turn of the century there have been major demographic changes in Big City. Retired people make up a large part of our present ridership – they're loyal, they tend to ride at off-peak hours, and use the service almost exclusively.

"Fully 32 percent of the population is over 65. Another 24 percent of the baby-boomers are reaching that age within five years. There are 25 percent more people with mobility challenges than just five years ago. And 26% of families are now living below the poverty line, according to the Big City Statistics Bureau's latest report.

"These people know their needs; our job is to find out more about those needs. We're looking forward to having them take part in the surveys because this is about re-building public transit to serve riders like them."

She had made core statements – pillar points, followed by a lot of 3-its, all backed by lots of hard statistics that served to support her main pillar points. The numbers added credibility because everyone can relate to those statistics. Statistics made her look smart, informed, like an expert, Tom thought.

Whenever Tom rattled off some statistics, his Aunt Betty would say that he was one smart nephew, for an engineer.

Then it clicked for Tom. "They're **aware** statements. She's showing the public she is aware of the issue," he said out loud.

"Yes Tom," the instructor said. "And, she's also letting her audience know she **cares** about their needs, by mentioning them publicly, by saying she wants their input, and by using words like *'serve'*.

"She even reminds them that she's doing her *share*."

"Yes, I caught the *'our job'* and the *'working to meet the needs'*," Tom said. She'd combined **all** the techniques so flawlessly that Tom was inspired to make the following summary notes on his communicator...

Techniques when looking for ponies:

— *Contract, Control, Confine*

— *Remind, Repeat, Re-negotiate*

— *Support phrases: Bridges, Baits, Re-asks*

— *Speaking style: Personable, Approachable, Enthusiastic plus Firm, Polite, Decisive*

— *Power Pillars: Premise point, 3-it, Sparklers*

— *Answering questions based on Format, Content, Pre-existing opinions*

"I can see why SPIN College chose Tanya as the model for their CSP," thought Tom.

There were systems to follow in order to deliver a successful message. When faced with a challenge, you had to follow the system and use the right tools. If you did, you ended up with a pretty strong structure.

And guess what appeared in the 'news' the next day…

Chapter 14

Headline News

Five Dollars
Weather: Heat Wave

Big City Bugle

May 29, 2012

New transit routes and schedules to be brought in within a year

You've been Zonked!
—by Dennis Zonk

It's time to get ready to be counted.

Consultations begin soon on Big City Transit's expansion program and the studies "will serve workers, businesses and consumers" according to BCT spokesperson Tanya Merkle.

BCT is looking at over 20 potential locations for new transit hubs, a huge undertaking. The amalgamation will bring together seven existing transit systems, operating over 22,000 square kilometres.

Merkle said the process will result in an energy-efficient, customer-oriented system designed to serve all of Big City.

When asked about fares, Merkle was clear about the issue.

"Fares are the final stage of the consultation. First, we have to work on some recommendations about routes and schedules. That will involve a survey that every resident in Big City is invited to complete whether they use transit or not.

"Next, we'll look at equipment needs. Then, once we know about capital improvement costs we will be able to discuss fares."

Equipment replacement is vital as many consider the current rolling stock of buses, streetcars and subways to be so outdated as to be potentially unsafe.

New transit system will serve workers, businesses, consumers.

Noting the changing transit needs of a rapidly aging population and the rising demand among the self- employed, Merkle said, "New transit routes and new schedules are to be brought in within a year."

Highlighting some of the innovations BCT was using, Merkle cited the new "employer-backed survey system". BCT is working in tandem with Big City Industries in the Big City Industrial Park, to provide time off for more than 22,000 employees in the area to complete their ridership surveys. BCT is open to all kinds of ideas for cooperation, at last.

This new openness on the part of BCT is a welcome change. Seems they have learned from mistakes of the past and are willing to share in the consultation process with those affected the most —my readers.

Let's get out there and help her. Let's get on board and be surveyed. If Ms. Merkle can follow through on her big plans, we stand to gain in a big way, readers. But if she can't follow through, we'll be watching.

One mistake, Ms. Merkle, and you're Zonked.

Keeping an eye out for management incompetence everywhere, I'm Dennis Zonk, standing up for you.

Chapter 15

Controversy: Which Side Are You On?

Finding common ground:

Controversial words

Extreme words

Common sense words

Plus: Looking at triangles

Tom realized that a news reporter could take almost any topic or issue and turn it into controversy.

There were three main participants in controversy and he thought of it as a triangle. He was an engineer, after all.

There were those who create controversy — like politicians, issues groups and the news media.

Most news stories are adversarial — one side pitted against another, highlighting some aspect of conflict. The conflict helps make it newsworthy.

Often there was a good guy/gal and a bad guy/gal — or someone trapped into looking bad.

There was sometimes an oversimplification into right-wing or left-wing definitions when the reality was somewhere in between. It's easy for the media to find controversial people.

Then, there were those who were victimized by controversy — usually bureaucrats, middle managers who weren't able to take advantage of an opportunity. Some couldn't see an advantage if they walked into one.

And thirdly, there are those who sought to benefit from controversy by turning it into a profit-making, issue-supporting or career-enhancing opportunity.

Tom preferred the career-enhancing opportunity that could turn potential controversy into publicity for the upcoming survey. He was being public-spirited.

Tom framed his thoughts in a 3-it model.

Controversy

Those who create it for their purposes:

- The News Media
- Politicians
- Issues groups or self-interests

Those who become victims of it:

- The guilty
- The innocent
- Bureaucratic scapegoats

Those who create opportunities from it:

- For self benefit
- For public benefit
- For unseen benefits

Tom took the main concepts and formed a triangle.

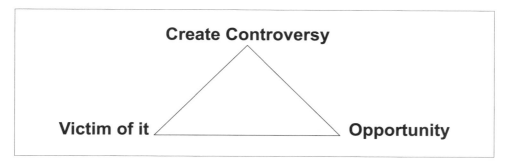

Now, Tom thought, "Where might a politician fit in this diagram? Where would various issues groups fit? Where would I fit in?"

His instructor saw the triangle, and challenged Tom. "Aren't those who **create** controversy at the **opposite** end of those who are **victims** of it? The opposite ends are **extremes**. Extremes are controversial because they're fraught with **emotions**, and they're **arguable**. If you say something is the best anything, someone will argue that it's the worst thing ever. It's spin, remember.

"You wouldn't want to position yourself as the worst spokesperson or the best spokesperson, but maybe you'd like to be seen as an articulate spokesperson, a helpful spokesperson, or an available spokesperson.

"Don't you really want to be in the middle, finding the ponies, the opportunities in controversy? Finding ways to get your message out? Let's look at it another way…"

The instructor drew a new, inverted triangle.

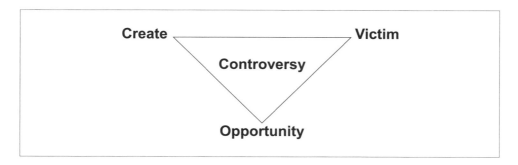

Tom wanted to take every *opportunity* to get his message out.

"Let me elaborate," the instructor said, drawing another triangle. "What if I asked you whether you think you're doing an **excellent** job or a **horrible** job? Or are you doing a pretty good job, or merely fair?"

Tom didn't find any of those words to be suitable.

The instructor agreed. "There are extreme sides, but the words **horrible** and **excellent** are **subjective**. They're emotion-based. And, they're **arguable**.

"But why would you choose to argue? Don't you want people to know you're doing a **thorough** job, a **comprehensive** job, or a **detailed** job? These words are **measurable** and **provable**, especially when they're backed up by a 3-it and lots of sparkling examples. Well, at least three," the instructor said, winking.

"You'll find that **neutral** words are **common-sense** words and they'll help put you on neutral or **common** ground, Tom. Let's illustrate it on this triangle."

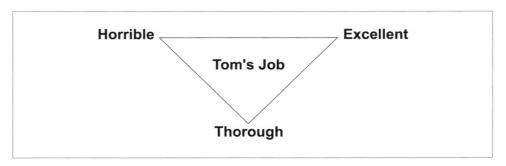

"Now make a pillar statement about your job using your neutral but provable word. Then, add your proving statements to form a Power Pillar that will serve as your **core message**. It might sound like this…

*"Tom Lee has a **thorough** job to do on the new transit initiative. He's **working with** 975 community groups, 44,200 employers and millions of transit riders. He's **evaluating** 19,265 routes, 87,900 pieces of equipment and all citizens' needs. He's **studying** how we did it in the past and how we do it now so that we can plan it better for the future."*

"Pillar point in neutral, inarguable language, supported by three sets of threes with lots of statistics. Nice simple package," Tom thought.

As an engineer, he loved structure. He was constantly challenged to look at new wording, phrasing or positioning.

He remembered the old saying about highway safety — Safety combines *engineering, enforcement and education.* How could he apply such a structured approach to an issue like red-light cameras at intersections, a very hot topic he had dealt with way back in the nineties?

The instructor invited Tom to turn the E's into C's. Instead of *Engineering,* think of *Construction* (always an inconvenience to drivers if not an outright controversy). Instead of *Enforcement,* think of *Cops.*

The final words could be edited later; this is only a structure, not a final message. It's a basic, simple **triad building block** that is easy to build onto.

Instead of talking about *Educating* drivers, he urged Tom to look at the issue as one of *Compliance* or obeying the law.

"Your real goal is more than education — it's getting others to do their part.

"That's pretty non-controversial and puts you into neutral common ground. It places far more emphasis on driver responsibility, and re-directs the issue to what drivers should do.

"Any messaging could then focus on asking drivers to obey the law. *Fewer people would be killed at intersections if drivers stopped at red lights.* No one could argue with that, Tom.

"When you find the common ground, and when you use neutral language to frame your inarguable premise of safety, you also avoid the emotion-based opposites."

Then Tom created a triangle to depict the issue and outlined some of the roles of each participant.

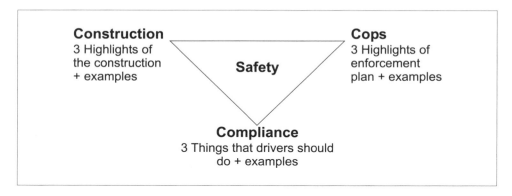

"Tom, let's combine it all here. You've got a core safety message ready, and I ask you what the construction office thinks about the police enforcement. *Are the police doing their share?* "

"The answer might start by acknowledging that the police have a plan and are available to talk about it. Your focus is on the three construction highlights, and you're also asking the public to do their share. *'That's why we're asking drivers to obey speed limits, stay a safe distance behind other cars, and stop at red lights. Safety starts at the wheel.'*

"Here's another favourite question: We call this the Goldilocks triangle. *Are you doing enough to deal with the issue of delays?* "

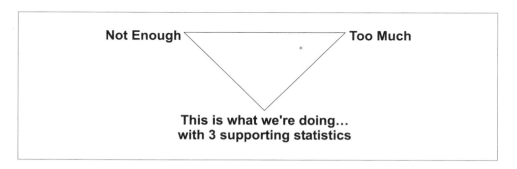

"Let the recipient of the message decide if you're doing enough, based on what you are doing. You will have at least 3 statistics and 3 stories to illustrate what you are doing, won't you, Tom?"

"So, if I need more staff or more money for my project," Tom answered, "I shouldn't start crying about not having enough staff?"

"Responsible public servants prove and show why they need staff or resources — without having to create a crisis. Crying for more staff without proving it went out of style long ago," said the instructor.

"If you need more resources, make your case based on a strategic, fact-filled description of the situation: the staff you have and what they're doing with the resources they have.

"Let the recipient of the information come to the obvious conclusion based on the way you've presented the facts.

"If you can't make the factual, logical and public-spirited case for more resources, you don't deserve them."

More Controversy

As Tom was preparing to launch the first transit users public meeting, a political bombshell hit. At least it hit the SPIN College classroom, not the real world. Tom found it hard to tell the difference sometimes.

Presumably, the former Mayor had learned that the costs for the public consultation were set at six million dollars. Her Worship, with an obvious agenda of her own, said that six million dollars could feed every hungry child in her home area of the city, for a year.

She called the survey outlay a "glossy public relations exercise" and "way out of line." She called it "a cover-up to deflect attention away from Transit's other issues, and an effort to sidetrack the news media." Everybody has their own spin.

"OK Tom, the first negative message is the term *glossy public relations exercise.* That's a sensationalized term designed to trap you into answering with a denial. How would you respond?"

"I would want to deny it, because it's not true," Tom said. "Or, I could refuse to comment on budget issues. Or, I would challenge the reporter and argue my point."

"By denying the allegation, Tom, you're really begging them to quote your denial. Saying **'No comment'** will make you sound guilty. And if you argue, you'd sound like a lawyer, which is fine in the context of a courtroom. Here, you have to think like a professional media spokesperson and like a customer service provider.

"With a customer, you want to avoid an emotion-based argument or disagreement.

"Take yourself out of the confrontation for a while and think about the bigger issue. Ask yourself what the question is about. How would you define the question so that it gives you an opportunity to explain and inform?

"All complex, trap and hostile questions contain within them an opportunity, Tom. Look for the easiest and simplest pony."

Tom thought a moment and then said, "The issue in this question is really about money, isn't it? Money's usually the biggest issue with politicians."

"You're real close Tom, let's just define it with even more neutral language — it's about costs. Now state your message about costs — say what you intend to say.

"Alright, once again from the top," the instructor said, taking on the role of a reporter.

"Mr. Lee, how would you respond to the Mayor's claim that your project is a waste of money and a glossy public relations exercise?"

Tom's answer started with a slight, but obvious pause, just long enough to think about the question, breathe in deeply and focus on going to message. The pause also sent a signal to the reporter, politely.

Tom smiled broadly, inhaled deeply and said sincerely:

> *"Big City Transit's consultation survey will cost nearly six million dollars.*
>
> *"That money is being spent to **help** over 7 million regular transit users, another 4 million potential users, and thousands of businesses.*

*"That money is being spent to **help** hundreds of organizations effectively plan their future transit needs.*

*"That money is being spent to see how **costs can be saved** if we **do this right**.*

"Let me give you an example of what some of the project costs will go toward.

*"Our Central Station information centre will **cost** $357,000.*

*"Our surveys will have an initial **cost** of $412,000. It will actually **save** $239,000 compared to…"*

The answer was purposely strong, neutral and structured to take control of the issue by defining it as one of costs. The definition of the issue was written in inarguable, common sense language.

It was designed to rise above the question and send a powerful signal that: "This project has a budget, we're spending it, and here's what we're spending it on. It will **help people and save money**."

Tom would let the recipient of his message decide if the money was being wasted or not. His answer disproved the inflammatory premise in the question with facts.

It was rich with statistics: Seven million transit users, four million potential users, thousands of businesses and hundreds of organizations will have a chance to plan **their** future transit needs.

That's a lot of newspaper readers or TV viewers, Tom realized.

His message positioned the issue squarely in the interests of a great number of people. The whole message is written in MediaSpeak style. It's written in the third person plural. It's about them, not us or me.

Tom smiled, and then he **spontaneously** bridged to a sparkler. At least it looked spontaneous. An instructor said that the key to a media encounter was the appearance of spontaneity. It meant moving quickly to your planned, intended message by volunteering new information.

"Let me give you an example of what some of the project costs will go toward."

He also made his message tantalizing, taking greater control of the encounter by baiting the reporter into gathering details, when he added, "Our survey will actually save money." *(Stop. Wait for it. You've thrown out the bait. Wait another second or even two seconds. Here it comes…)*

Question: "Save money? I don't believe it. How will it do that?"

What else could someone ask?

Answer: "Our corporate partners paid for the advertising of the survey. That alone saved us more than $2,000,000. That money will go towards …"

When you suddenly start talking about saving money, you've really re-defined the issue for the consumer, who wants costs to go down. You have raised the issue yourself, and most reporters will take the bait.

Follow-up question: "So are you suggesting that the Mayor is playing politics with this issue? As a professional engineer, do you object to this meddling by the Mayor just as your program is about to start?"

The questioner was sticking to trap-style questions, ignoring Tom's role. This interview needed some re-negotiating in the middle of itself.

Tom came up with this answer: "Let's look at the numbers. There are over seven million regular transit users, millions of former transit users, and many more potential transit users. They all need to be heard from. Some of the ways we're trying to reach them include survey forms and even an on-line survey. We're encouraging everyone to *'Get on board'* and do the survey."

He'd begun with a bridging phrase:

▶ Let's look at the numbers.

He continued with a 3-it:

▶ There are over seven million regular transit users,
▶ millions of former transit users,
▶ and even more potential transit users.

Then, an inarguable pillar:

▶ They all need to be heard from.

Next, a sparkler explaining one of the steps they were taking:

▶ Some of the ways we're trying to reach them include survey forms and even an on-line survey.

And he finished by telling the reporter what they were asking the public to do, using his now-famous slogan:

▶ We are encouraging everyone to *'Get on board'* and do the survey.

The instructor lobbed a third question: "So what do you think motivates the Mayor? Is this an attempt at headline grabbing at your expense?"

Tom wanted to remind the questioner what he was there to talk about.

"I'm able to answer questions about the benefits, timelines and costs of this consultation project. That's really my area of expertise. I'd be pleased to answer questions about those things."

He'd just renegotiated the contract mid-stream. He had gently but firmly reminded the reporter what he could talk about — which was what they'd agreed to talk about.

He repeated his role statements whenever the reporter got off-track.

Then he bridged quickly back to his main message.

"Let me tell you about some of the mobile display equipment we'll be taking to our community workshops."

He was getting more comfortable using yet another bridge to yet another sparkler. He was becoming enthusiastic. He was starting to enjoy it a bit.

"At our kiosks, we'll be providing electronic downloading systems so passengers can enter their travel plans directly or do the survey at home.

"You just call up the screen to map out your travel needs and the computer enters the information into the survey database as you answer simple questions.

"It's really fun, come on over here and I'll show you how it works…"

If, at this stage the instructor/reporter had continued to ask about the politician, he'd be exhibiting repetitive behaviour.

Tom would have chosen the best response — to become repetitive in his answers, just like Tanya.

He'd learned a lot from SPIN College's CSP.

Chapter 16

Big City Takes A Survey

Tom handles questions involving:

Speculation

Personal opinions

Reacting to others

It all comes together:

He builds solid media relations

He smiles on live TV

He goes for results

Big City Transit would kick off the massive survey at a special ceremony at the Central Station information centre. The media would be present.

Big City TV was to broadcast the opening live and report on the initial survey results as they streamed in. The results would be displayed on a giant map about an hour after the survey opened to the public.

As part of the kick-off TV coverage, the program producers would be inviting over a hundred representatives from community organizations for interviews and to participate in discussions while waiting for the early survey results to appear at the information centre. They asked Tom to appear live and answer questions.

Tom was hesitant to take part at first, until he realized that these were all groups whose cooperation was needed. If they wanted their views known, they could do it by encouraging their members to do the survey. The more people surveyed, the better the results, he told them.

Tom's main job in the live TV program would be to analyze the data as it started to appear. His goal was to use the kick-off as a way to encourage people to participate in the survey, even if they were not among those on the first day.

The news coverage in advance of the kick off had been both positive and negative. The awareness level was huge — that is, everywhere you went you saw advertising messages to *'Get on board'.*

He anticipated that the main media questions would be about participation rates:

> ▶ How many people would even bother with the survey?

> ▶ What if the participation rate was low?

> ▶ Would the data still be useful?

> ▶ What happened if... If... If...

Tom wanted his messages to avoid speculation in all those *ifs*. He was prepared to turn every question into an opportunity to go to message.

He was ready to talk about the actual results from the Big Cities formerly known as Los Angeles, Tokyo and London. In the past 18 months, Tom had helped those cities conduct similar surveys. He compared the survey participation rates to the most recent voter turnout rates in elections. Then these rates were further compared to the city's transit ridership rates.

Tokyo's voting rate was high, at over 80%, and their survey participation rate was 79%. About 80% of the public used transit daily, due to Tokyo's limitations on private vehicles.

London's voting rate was about 60% and the survey rate was 67%. London loved its transit system, at least the way it had been before climate change caused the floods of 2008. Their ridership levels were about 63%.

Los Angeles had a voting rate of 27%, about the same as many cities in the former USA. The ridership levels in the city of freeways were a dismal 13%. But their survey participation rate was a surprising 40%. Although bigger than the voter turnout, it was still less than a majority of the population. The auto lobby, the energy industry and some politicians would challenge a result of less than 50%, Tom knew.

Tom's Big City had a voting rate of 59%, and a ridership rate of 57%. Everybody, it seemed, used the data selectively from the other cities for their own purposes, and it was mostly all speculation.

It was easy for the experts to compare Big City to Los Angeles because there were some demographic similarities. Los Angeles had never had a strong public transit system, and Big City did have decent, not bad, transit. All comparisons could be dangerous, Tom knew. For about a week he fended off speculative questions by sticking to his message, stating statistics and urging everyone to **'Get on board'** and do the survey.

Tom was the only person not speculating on the survey outcome. He had made notes in his communicator and brought them to every interview. There were far too many facts, figures and statistics to remember. Once he learned to glance at his notes like a reporter, he felt less self-conscious about reading.

That way, he wouldn't have to say, *"I can't speculate on that."*

Two weeks before the kick-off, Big City Transit upped the stakes. Big City Industries signed on as an official partner in the transit riders' survey. They donated prizes — 1100 leather jackets with built-in personal communicators and anti-theft security upgrades in the jacket lining.

The jackets would be individually tailored for each winner, using data stored on their personal communicator. They were featured on all of Big City Transit's marketing messages in every bus, streetcar, subway car, shared car, truck, taxi — even on the share-ride bicycles that dotted the city.

The first 1,000 people who completed the survey could win one of the jackets. The remaining 100 jackets would be awarded randomly throughout the day. It was the best marketing idea of the year for the giant manufacturer.

If some reporters asked if the sudden marketing push was a desperate act, Tom had his answer ready: "It is a good marketing opportunity and it's also a great reminder to *'Get on board'* and do the survey on opening day."

Finally the survey day arrived and Big City watched the results live on TV.

Here's a written excerpt from parts of the TV program **Big City Today**. Meet the *new* Tom Lee.

(Opening shot: Wide pan of Central Station showing about 400 invited guests watching a giant electronic map of Big City. Microphones pick up conversation buzz, over which we hear the...)

Announcer's voice: "We interrupt our regular programming for a special presentation. History is being made today in Big City and we're there. We're live at Central Station where Big City Transit is launching its ridership survey. We're about to *'Get on board'*. Our host, Emma Bender is standing by. Emma."

Emma: "Good morning Big City. History is being made here in Central Station. As you can see from the crowd of people behind me, there's a big turnout for this event today. It all started 55 minutes ago when the public had their first chance to complete their transit needs surveys. All over Big City, thousands of workers have been given time off to *'Get on board'*.

"The crowd here today is pretty impressive. Almost everyone who's anyone is on hand for a new exercise in consumer democracy. We'll hear more of their views later, but now it's your views we want to hear. So, everyone, *'Get on board'* and complete your surveys."

(moves to giant Big City map)

"I'm standing in front of this massive map of Big City. Until a few minutes ago, the map was unlit, completely dark. Within just the last few minutes we've started to see a whole lot of lines all over the map. There are lots of different colours and it looks really confusing.

"Here to explain it all is Tom Lee, who is coordinating this survey. Tom, it looks like a dog's breakfast up there. What's happening?"

Tom Lee: "Good morning Emma. I'm delighted to be here. Let me tell you what's happening. Right now, the early survey results are being displayed individually. But this mass of individual lines is soon going to start changing and coming together as more surveys are completed.

"Our central computer is taking riders' individual information and applying it to a database of possible transit routes.

"These potential routes are among the hundreds of suggestions that have been made. We've entered all those proposed routes into a database. Now riders' individual needs are being matched up with those proposed new routes.

"Once the data is analyzed, the computer will show us the best possible routes on the map."

Emma: "You mean it's like voting for your own transit route?"

Tom Lee: "It's really about your individual needs.

"Say you want to travel every Friday night to bowling and you live here on Lakeshore Drive **(points to map)**, and want to get to Big City Lanes, here **(points to a different part of the map)**.

"Maybe the fastest way is along Beach Street, past the new Mellow Housing development. You'd have to go past the harbour but you could loop up near Olympic Avenue, past Saylor Lane. There seems to be some demand there.

"Once you enter the information, your Friday night needs will be combined with everyone else's. All the information will be applied to the transit system's future equipment needs. The more data we receive from the surveys, the more accurate the needs analysis will be."

Emma: "Sort of like the old computer games featuring simulated cities?"

Tom: "A lot like that only much easier. I have an 84-year-old aunt who called me this morning to brag that it only took her 9 minutes to do her survey. Here, let me show you how we'll link up the existing transit routes…" **(Shows more examples using the map)**

Emma: "There's been some concern about the feasibility of some routes. Can we really use the electrical power line corridors, the former rail lines and new bus routes together?"

Tom: "The computer has been programmed to consider all possibilities. It has information on every route, every study, every report, every recommendation ever made on possible routes in the past 25 years.

"As the individual surveys come in, the computer applies every need to thousands of possible routes.

"For instance..."

Emma: "Sorry to interrupt, Tom, but we have an update from reporter Jason Willow. We go now live to Jason who's at Big City Automotive. Over 2,000 employees have been given time off work to *'Get on board'*. Hi Jason, it looks pretty quiet there actually."

Jason: "Well, good morning Emma. It's actually very quiet now, but here are some views from about a half-hour ago. As you can see behind me in the main office area, it didn't take long for the 2,154 staff to finish.

"Let's see how one of those employees, Jennifer Cubinick, felt about doing the survey.

"What was it like Jennifer?"

Jennifer: "It was actually, like, fun, especially the part about the weekends. I like to go, like, to the racetrack, and I got to enter that in the survey. Maybe they'll, like, improve the rotten service to the track for us."

Jason: "Did you win a jacket by any chance?"

Jennifer: "No way, but my brother did. He's, like, at school and they all did the survey there the same time we did. It's like, an awesome jacket man."

Jason: "How long did it take you to do the survey, Jennifer?"

Jennifer: "Like, it only took me about 20 minutes."

Jason: "Not bad at all. Thanks for talking to us, Jennifer. Back to you in the control booth, Emma."

Emma: "Thanks Jason. This event is not without controversy. Tom, according to Janet Earl of the union of homemakers, this transit reorganization will ignore the needs of domestic engineers. Do you agree with Ms. Earl?"

Tom: "We know that many domestic engineers use transit for shopping, so we want to know what times and routes will work best for their needs. Say they work in DeCare Heights and want to shop at The Point Plaza, over here. The closest current stop is Rivers Station and you have to cross McKenzie Parkway to get there.

"The best thing about the survey is — the computer figures out the best route AND the fastest way to get there. The users don't have to worry about traffic lights, one-way streets or even construction. We think they'll find it really easy to do the survey at home, using their personal communicators."

Emma: "There's been a lot of speculation about turnout and we don't have any figures at all here. Are you afraid this may all turn out to be a glossy public relations exercise?"

Tom: "Well, as the report from Big City Automotive showed just now, it seems that a lot of people are taking part. We really need people's help today if we're to get going on future transit improvements. We really need people to tell us what their own needs are."

Emma: "What happens if the participation rate is below fifty percent, will you have failed?"

Tom glanced at his notes, preparing to answer, but before he could begin Emma cut him off again.

Emma: "We have an important question for you from a man in our audience who has asked us to conceal his face."

(Walks into the audience to a man wearing a paper bag on his head. He's over six feet tall and big. There are eye and mouth holes in the paper bag.)

Emma: "Our questioner is Dennis Zonk, of the Big City Bugle."

(Most of the crowd applauds wildly for the crusading columnist. A few boo and hiss.)

Emma: "Mr. Zonk, your question?"

Zonk: "Mr. Lee, BC Transit promised that it would be working on behalf of transit users with special mobility needs, such as wheelchair users and people who have a hard time getting around. Why have you ignored all their needs sir?"

Tom: "People's individual needs are the heart of this program. All travelers doing the survey are asked about any extra requirements. All travelers are asked about any current problems they encounter when using the system. We've asked for their help in identifying barriers to safe, clean and reliable transit.

"Let me show you some examples already in the survey database. The visually impaired have said they want better lighting, bigger signage and an increased use of Braille on the signage.

"People using wheelchairs tell us we have too many curbs at bus stops. And the residents of more than 16 seniors complexes have said enclosed shelters at streetcar stops would be a major improvement."

Zonk: "Why have you forgotten about the poor and the young — especially the students?"

Tom: "We have welcomed their input, and they weren't shy about giving it either. In fact, the students at Hawthorne High were the ones who let us know that we need more capacity on Route 808. We've also had input not only from all the school boards but also from teachers and parents groups, food banks and the Big City Coalition Against Poverty."

Emma: "Excuse me Tom, but our map is starting to change. It looks like some giant snakes are crawling all over Big City. What are we seeing now?"

Tom: "That's the computer's way of telling us that it has enough information to start making route suggestions. The results are pouring in now, and we'll have an actual figure soon. In just a moment we'll know how many people have done their survey. We're hoping for at least a million people, so let's see, here we are… Ummmmm, uhhhhhh"

(Numbers flash on screen.) Tom suddenly became tongue-tied. He couldn't seem to say anything. He was visibly blushing.

Emma: "It says 7.2. What does that mean?"

Tom: "Suh… Suh…SEVEN…"

Emma: "I'm sorry?"

Tom: (Recovering quickly) "It's supposed to mean 7.2 million people have done their survey, but that can't be right — not in the first hour!"

Emma: "Tom, I think it looks like we've made history. Big City is voting today for better public transit. In just 63 minutes, the number of surveys completed — 7,243,954!

"That's 7,243,954 people who have gotten on board.

"My gosh, that's more than 50% of all of Big City's population — in the first hour, Tom. Can this be right?"

Tom: "The technical experts can tell us that pretty quickly, but what's more exciting is this early data. We know from other cities that the initial survey data will give us real solid information. Look here." **(points to the zoo.)**

Emma: "What's this big line past the zoo mean?"

Tom: "That big line past the zoo could very well become a major new transit route linking the Big City World Airport with the western downtown. That route was recommended in one of last year's studies and today's survey shows there is a case to be made for diverting traffic away from…"

And for another hour, Tom's survey came together, with much of Big City watching. There were a few technical glitches, but none that Tom hadn't prepared for.

He'd been trained for an interview with the reporter from hell, and who shows up? Old Zonker himself.

'Zonk' wouldn't ever say it to Tom's face, but he admitted to himself that Tom had come a long way from their encounter that first day at SPIN College.

"He's learned how to take control, certainly. And he seems to have avoided my negative questions. I tried to trap him but he had a solid message about all the groups I mentioned. He even had 3 examples that supported what he said.

"Maybe I'll un-Zonk him in my next column.

"Yeah, right," he chuckled to himself. "Like that's gonna happen."

Chapter 17

Headline News

Big City Bugle

Big Company, Big Union, Big Egos

You've Been Zonked!
—by Dennis Zonk

How far is Big City Energy Services prepared to go in dealing with an out-of-control union? That's the question this week as we approach elections at BCES's amalgamated unions.

Bringing together all our city's utility services was a big job. Uniting their workforce will be even bigger.

The former cable companies had a workforce made up largely of self-employed private contractors.

The old telephone company had a mix of union and private sector contractors.

Workers are unionized, but the unions are subject to new regulations that take into account productivity standards, to which most employees wholeheartedly agreed.

Only the electrical workers still operate under the old union contracts, dating back to the 1940's.

Now, don't be misled, there are a few advantages to workers under the old system. One advantage for electrical workers, still called linemen (because most are still men) is known unofficially as the "Two-man rule." It states that two workers are to be assigned to each service call.

It was a good rule when it was created. The work was largely outdoors. It involved stringing heavy electric cable on poles.

Since then the work has changed dramatically, but the rules haven't. Today, many lines are underground, linked to alternate energy sources.

The two-man rule stands in the way of integration and it's being challenged by the workers in their executive elections. The present union leadership wants to retain the status quo. A new slate of candidates is seeking full integration.

Electing a new executive means a streamlined new utility service.

If the old executive is re-elected, it means a delay in improvements. We give them a big Zonk today.

Electing a new executive means a streamlined new utility service.

In past columns, I've uncovered a series of problems for the utility service. Consumers have been treated to the worst kind of service imaginable. Trying to arrange a service call is a nightmare, and once you get one, two burly technicians do finally show up, then often have to 'go back to the shop for a part', have to 'finish it up tomorrow' or can't fix what's wrong.

It's bad enough that service call charges tripled under privatization

It's bad enough that those high charges are still in place. It's bad enough that no one seems to care. But really bad service is a damn shame.

Zonk has learned of a secret plan to bring in better customer service programs. Despite repeated calls to BCES, we can't get a denial or confirmation. We're pleased, however, at the appointment of Tanya Merkle as BCES's VP of customer service.

In a recent interview, Ms. Merkle said that improvements are on the way "soon," and that more details would be available within "weeks."

Meanwhile, real people are getting hit badly with energy outages, power surges and slow service calls.

Memo to BCES: We're paying for this crap and we want you to fix it.

Memo to BCES workers: It's up to you.

So we say to the electrical workers voting next week on a new executive: vote for Big City's future. Vote for change.

Keep an eye out for management incompetence everywhere. Report union mismanagement here. You know how to reach me.

Standing up for better energy services. I'm Dennis Zonk.

Chapter 18

Tanya's Promotion

The real issues here are:

Improved customer service

Better safety for our workers

Savings for the customer

It was a Monday morning and Tanya Merkle woke up to the sounds of her personal communicator beeping. It was over a year since she'd first been turned into a cyber-spokesperson, CSP, at SPIN College and her real life had been pretty busy ever since.

That beeping, along with a red light, meant bad news for the new Vice President of Big City Energy Services — BCES.

It was the operations centre at SPIN College, alerting her to this morning's Dennis Zonk column about the massive utility. Tanya swore, but just a little. She laughed at herself for the language lapse.

She switched on her communicator's screen and read the Zonk piece. She kept cursing, and her swear words became less fashionable.

Tanya's job as VP of Customer Service at BCES depended on major changes to union contracts as they came up for review and union ratification. Once they were in place, BCES could roll out new programs to improve customer service.

When Tanya had been assigned to the job, plans were already underway to change from 2-person work crews to a new system, originally called *working alone* by the human resources branch.

Tanya had recommended that the program name be changed, from *working alone* to the more accurate — **work match**. It was better spin, she realized. She'd do even better soon.

Tanya was concerned about the Dennis Zonk column. It dealt so directly with problems among the service crews and with proposed changes in work assignments. Obviously Zonk had a few pipelines into the union's issues, but Tanya was restricted in what she could say publicly about the union.

She was under strict orders not to discuss labour-management issues surrounding customer service changes. She'd been instructed not to talk about the unions, the union elections, or internal problems within the union executive. Elections were under way for new union leaders and the company did not want to be seen as interfering.

Her focus was on improving customer services, and her plans and messages were already well developed. She had to start bringing them all together if she needed to act quickly on the fall-out from this column.

Tanya called SPIN College and spoke to her mentor and coach, George Olds.

He'd seen the Zonk column and suggested she prepare for all hell to break loose. SPIN's advice for Tanya was to hold off saying much today, other than, "The negotiations are continuing, and the company is looking forward to new ways of delivering services."

George added, "I thought you should know that there's going to be a letter to the editor in tomorrow's paper that blows the lid off the work crew issue, or at least it could if you don't address it. I got a copy of the letter in advance; don't ask me how.

"We've already drawn up a list of potential horror questions. I'm sending them to you now, along with a copy of the letter to the editor of the **Big City Bugle**. When you need to get back to us, let me know."

Tanya replied, "If your questions have covered the bases, I can take it from there. I hope you were gentle."

Tanya set to work reading the letter. *"What a blessing to have 24 hours notice,"* she thought. Or was this maybe, just maybe… No it couldn't be, could it?

Was this possibly one of George's tests? She remembered his class on *writing letters to the editor* as a way of influencing public opinion. *"#@*&! him."*, she thought.

No matter, she got to work studying the letter that just might appear in tomorrow's paper. George had a good track record at getting his letters published, she remembered. His workshop had been fun, too.

The letter addressed many issues in 6 simple paragraphs.

Dear Editor,

My spouse is being forced to risk his life as a result of a secret plan by Big City Energy Services to slash work crews to one worker only, an evil, secret, dangerously-devised plan called working alone. It should be called <u>Dying Alone</u>, because that's what will happen.

Imagine the scene, brave workers all alone on the line, lying in the cold, freezing to death or electrified after millions of volts of power run through them and there's no one to help.

As a smokescreen, management at BCES have had the audacity to accuse our energy workers of abusing overtime, after their hard and dangerous work during last year's ice storms where people almost froze to death. These guys saved lives and worked around the clock. BCES is bashing heroes.

This from some fat-cat executive earning $865,000 a year while our kids wear second-hand clothes!!! BCES claims this is a move to improve service, but I ask: at what cost? Shame on them.

I'm calling today on the Workers Safety Board to halt this dreadful plan before innocent lives are lost as a sacrifice to corporate greed.

I'm also calling on the BCES Owners Council next week to reject management's blackmail demands for a 9 percent rate increase. Stop this insanity!!!

Marge Tanner
601 Main Street
Big City

As Tanya read the letter, her heart sank. "The cat's out of the bag now," she thought. She knew Marge Tanner. Marge Tanner was no friend of hers. Marge Tanner was the domestic partner of Ommar Phannu, vice president of the union. "This letter might be real."

She set to work.

She looked at George's horror questions and came up with a plan to deal with the questions and issues in the letter to the editor. She first had to:

> ▶ Find, then redefine the issues and negative messages contained in the letter and anticipate the horror questions that might be asked by anyone.

▶ Develop or update her core messages consisting of pillars, supports and sparklers, starting with Power Pillars and 3-it statements.

▶ Determine what new material she would need in the way of backgrounders or sparklers, and where she would get the necessary information.

George's Negative Question #1: "How pervasively has **greed** permeated into the very fibre of your company? Are you prepared to **sacrifice the lives** of your workers for the **bottom line**?"

Tanya saw this was a bombshell question designed to throw her off message and make her defensive.

She pictured a potentially negative headline:

BCES denies greed in dangerous plan

She had to move quickly and decisively to position and re-define the issues.

Her response had to be positioned in the greatest public (customer) interest.

Her present message had to be based on an inarguable premise, supported by details and examples.

Her inarguable premises, or common-sense definitions:

▶ improving customer service,
▶ reducing the costs of service calls and, of course,
▶ safety.

Service, savings and safety. Service, savings and safety. Service, savings and safety.

She would repeat the three inarguable premises to herself often as a little reminder.

She remembered her SPIN College core skills:

▶ Take control of the interview encounter by avoiding defensiveness.
▶ Re-define the negative words in the question.
▶ Structure a response for format.

She started by de-constructing George's horror question, to determine its simplest core.

Question: "How pervasively has greed permeated into the very...?"

She simplified the negative question:

Are you motivated by greed?

She simplified it some more:

What motivates you?

Answer:

▶ *Service*
▶ *Safety*
▶ *Savings*

Here are her opportunity questions, the ponies, in this bombshell:

▶ What are you doing? *Improving service*

▶ Why are you doing this? *Savings and safety*

▶ How are you doing this? *A comprehensive safety program.*

Then she needed bridging phrases to move to the ponies:

▶ *Let me be very clear about why we're improving our customer service work and how we're planning to reduce costs.*
(Deals with what's being done and why.)

▶ *Let me tell you why we're making changes, and how safety concerns are such an important part of our work.*
   (Deals with why and how.)

▶ *Let's look at some of the changes we're making to reduce the costs of service and reduce our emergency response times.*
   (Deals with what and how.)

Tanya reviewed some of her existing pillar statements. She had reams of material on the topic and she had some terrific sparklers. She practised some possible pillars out loud…

BCES is working to improve customer service, safely.

That's why we're changing the way we carry out job assignments for our work crews.

The new work-match project will mean quicker response times for service calls, reduced costs and improved worker safety.

BCES cares deeply about our workers' safety. That's why this work-match project will include new technology, new job assessment techniques and new training for all workers.

Tanya had a terrific sparkler she could volunteer very early in an encounter. It would be part of the upcoming announcements, but she'd ask her boss about releasing the details if the letter to the editor appeared. She could use this sparkler to deflect the issue toward customer service improvements.

One of the things we're doing is introducing a whole new customer service response team. It's called the **Come-Back Squad**.

They're a specialized team of 418 recently retired technical staff, working from their homes. They can help customers with needs ranging from service outages to home appliance repairs.

When you call for help, you'll get an experienced service technician who can help you promptly.

All you need to do when you call is take your personal communicator and attach it to your electrical panel.

That way, the technician can run an energy audit that involves…

GNQ #2: "How soon do you expect the Safety Board to cancel this horrific, dangerous project, or do you personally think that maybe Claire Evans is playing politics with this issue?"

"Omygawwwd," was all Tanya could think.

"George must have written this one before his reconstituted, simulated, coffee-type beverage product. We've got a sudden and very specific trap-filled reference to the Safety Board, and its publicity-prone chairwoman."

Claire Evans was a supporter of the Mayor, too.

Spotting the *speculative personal opinion trap* was easy for Tanya. She offered the opinion that "The real issue is safety here."

No way could she talk about the *Safety Board* unless they became directly involved, and she certainly did not want to say anything that would rattle Chair Claire Evans or cause her to suddenly become involved because of what appeared in the media.

Tanya knew there was a pony in this question, and she prepared several messages to bring it out of the stable, so to speak.

Safety has been our main concern since we began the work-match project two years ago.

▶ *That's why we introduced new training programs for our 39,000 workers.* Three highlights of that program are _____, _____ and _____.

▶ *That's why we've made adjustments to thousands of work procedures.* These adjustments include _____, _____ and _____.

▶ *That's why we're providing workers with new communications equipment, such as…".* (Show new equipment; demonstrate, if required)

That seemed solid. She'd just have to fill in the blanks with the actual facts, figures and statistics later. She continued making notes.

Our work-match training programs include:

▶ *a week in the classroom.*
  (If needed, she could add three highlights of classroom training.)

▶ *a month on the work-site.*
  (three features or benefits of work-place training)

▶ *25 years of experience from other utility companies who've improved their service.* (three examples of experiences learned from other utilities)

New procedures have been brought in to deal with:

▶ *how we assess the work that needs to be done.* (Explain details for new assignment sheets — three highlights of the new forms.)

▶ *how we establish priorities.* (Outline an example of priority assignments from a typical weekend. List three situations with varying priority, all based on safety, service and protecting the environment.)

▶ *how we assign the safest number of workers to handle each job.* (based on feedback from the **Come Back Squad**)

She made a note to call the Operations Coordinator (Come Back Squad) for extra information on:

▶ Work assessment — three main ways to assess need.
▶ Work priorities — three main priorities such as hospital or other emergencies, residential and corporate.
▶ Work assignment — three steps to assigning work crews.

New equipment is being brought in to improve safety:

▶ *Workers will be provided with dedicated responder units,*
▶ *new electronic back-up equipment, and*
▶ *new facilities at our Riverdale control centre.*

She added a few more sound-bite statements bordering on clichés.

At BCES, we're giving our workers the tools, the procedures and the training to do their jobs safely.

At BCES, safety can create savings and improve service.

If she was pressed on Safety Board issues, she would stress the expertise of the team who'd worked two years on the plan.

They included Dr. Isobel MacKay, author of *Workplace Safety in Big City,* and Heather Chow, BCES consumer safety director. Tanya had 150-word One Minute Power Messages on each of them, and they'd both graduated from SPIN College.

If she was really pressed about the safety board and if, repeat, **if** it looked like the board were suddenly interested, Tanya would offer to hold a meeting with them as soon as possible to brief them fully.

She didn't know how the Chair of the Safety Board would react to a media opportunity, so Tanya would have her media monitoring software tuned to any word from Ms. Claire Evans or her office.

GNQ #3: "According to a recent letter to the editor, you're sending workers out into dangerous situations. Will it take the death of a worker to reverse this policy, or are you prepared to sit idly by and allow workers to be electrocuted? Do you agree with the letter writer?"

Now what's George doing? This is too easy, she thought. *"Do I agree with her? Come on man."*

As soon as she spotted the word *dangerous,* Tanya saw the same pony as the previous question. She could repeat a core safety message or two, but then she needed to really deal with the work-scheduling issue on an emotional level. She needed a Power Pillar that summed it all up and it needed to feel really good inside when she said it.

It came to her quickly, and as soon as the thought struck, she knew it would work. She wondered why the message hadn't hit her earlier. Because she was so close to this issue, she realized she hadn't always been seeing the forest for the trees. Tanya found that a little bit of pressure did marvels for her creativity. She'd noticed that in a few of her instructors, too.

She wrote down one of those special sound-bites or quotable quotes that could sum up the issue very succinctly.

Later, her boss told her that this one statement was good enough to justify her salary for a year:

Let me tell you about work-matching:

▶ *When the job requires 7 workers to do it safely, we'll send 7.*
▶ *When the job requires 12, we'll send 12.*
▶ *And when the job only requires one worker to achieve safety, we'll send one.*

▶ **We're working to improve customer service and keep costs down.**

Tanya developed sparkling examples about sending out a huge emergency truck with two great big workers to change a little utility meter, or sending out one technician in a solar-powered mini-car to do the same job.

Vehicles ranged in size from a $2,000,000. Sky HOOK Explorer, down to the 2-person, environmentally responsible, $15,000. mini-car now in use at BCES.

If necessary, she would insist on conducting TV interviews standing in front of various vehicles to illustrate her point. Not once, however, would she talk about the present union negotiations. If she had to play tough, she could do it with *service, savings,* and *safety.*

GNQ #4: "What about the suggestion that you're forcing workers to risk their lives and destroy their families in this dangerous venture? To what degree is this new policy an effort to destroy the unions, or is this just another attack on the labour movement in Big City?"

He wasn't letting up easily. Tanya was under strict orders to stay away from any union issues. That was all her boss had told her. She knew she must not get drawn into any questions that would impact on the current negotiations.

She opted to go with a *content-filled* message about the work-match program. She knew it inside-out. Since she'd been at BCES, it had been key to fixing the customer service mess. Customer service levels could not have been worse.

Under the work-match project, BCES will assign one worker only to jobs such as those involving:

▶ *customer-owned equipment.*
(Explain carefully with examples.)
▶ *certain streetlight repairs.*
(Explain carefully with examples.)
▶ *electric meter replacements.*
(Explain carefully with demonstration.)

GNQ #5: "How about you fat-cat overpaid executives? You've given yourselves huge wage increases when the rest of the company's salaries are frozen at 2010 levels."

"Oh, Olds is really starting to slow down," she thought. BCES had tons of background documents and official messages on this issue.

They'd been through this one before. It comes up around the time of the hearings into rate increases. The board set the salaries, but the question was an attempt to muddy the safety issue and sidetrack the spokesperson.

BCES had brought in an executive compensation specialist to carry out comparison salary studies in similar organizations, and all of the core messages were ready to roll at the upcoming hearings.

Tanya would use some of these messages if she needed them to deal with the letter to the editor. She practised one.

Compensation levels are clearly and repeatedly shown to be fair:

▶ *They're fair to executives, fair to our shareholders and fair within the industry.*
▶ *They're based on comparison salaries in positions at industries like ...*

Once she'd dealt with the issue of compensation, she would sum up with:

▶▶ *This new work-match program is designed to improve customer service.*

GNQ #6: "Are you drumming up support for a big rate increase at next month's rate hearings at the expense of your workers? How can you justify a 9% increase when new energy sources are coming online that are cheaper?"

She had pages and pages of message backgrounders ready for the rate hearings.

▶▶ The proposed rate increase is largely due to a 12% environmental surcharge on utility bills.

▶▶ The surcharge is part of Big City's commitment to the ongoing Kyoto climate change action plan.

▶▶ Protecting the environment is our responsibility.

The company was actually reducing their part of the bill by 3%. Details would be outlined at the upcoming hearings. Tanya would want to focus on some of the larger issues facing the new utility at the hearings.

The purpose of the rate hearings is to give BCES the opportunity to:

▶▶ *improve service,*
▶▶ *fund capital projects, and*
▶▶ *protect the environment.*

She pulled up some notes.

▶▶ 3 customer service improvements,

▶▶ 3 capital projects that are planned or underway, and

▶▶ 3 important developments in protecting the environment — wind turbines, alternate fuels, air cleaners.

GNQ #7: "We hear it's been pretty messy at the bargaining table. Our sources say that management is in a knot about overtime and they've made some serious allegations about abuse. How dare you accuse workers of abusing overtime when they slaved during last year's storm?"

He'd hit a hot button issue here.

This was a big issue in the current labour negotiations, but so far they had managed to keep it from the public.

Tanya knew that once the overtime cat was out of the bag, she'd have no choice but to *ventilate the issue* of overtime — with facts and numbers on costs, hours, improvements identified. She was ready for the questions whenever her boss thought it might help them at the bargaining table. Timing would be everything here, she knew.

She could provide pages and pages of details to illustrate the overtime situation as a very high-cost issue. Work-match would cut overtime, but ice storms were very expensive.

She could, if necessary, explain how much was spent last year on overtime ($617 million) and what steps are being proposed to reduce overtime costs without pointing any fingers at the workers.

She'd be taking the position that, yes, overtime costs were very high last year, for safety reasons.

Overtime is necessary in the utility business:

▶▶ *It's necessary for the safety of our workers on big jobs where extra help is needed.*
▶▶ *Overtime is sometimes necessary in order to serve our customers quickly.*
▶▶ *We also recognize that it's necessary to reduce the cost of overtime wherever we can to keep rates down.*

Work-match will improve customer service and help keep costs down.

She added a few more talking points and potential sound-bite slogans.

> *In every area we serve, from _____ to _____ and from _____ to _____ , our workers are _____.*

> *Our workers care about their jobs. They know they're serving their neighbours, their communities and the economy of this city every time they do their work.*

> *We're giving our workers the tools, the skills and the training to get the job done quickly and safely, and at the same time reduce costs for our customers.*

> *Work-match will improve service with safety as its main priority and savings as a result.*

Tanya knew that if the overtime issue became hot, she had some reports and studies from consultants supporting the company's moves. It wouldn't be too difficult for a copy of the reports to reach a reporter. All Tanya had to do was call a certain board member or two, and say verrrry discreetly, *"Whatever you do, make sure those overtime reports don't get into the hands of the media."*

If she said that, some reporter would have them in about five minutes. Tanya had used this method before, although the board member never knew what Tanya was really doing.

That was it, seven questions.

Tanya went back through the letter to the editor. *Would it actually appear tomorrow, or was this one of George's tests,* she wondered.

Within 90 minutes, Tanya had gone through the horror questions, reviewed her answers and decided what follow-up action was needed.

With her core messages updated and her task list prepared, Tanya contacted her team members who would serve as possible back-up spokespersons on technical issues. She asked them to develop some potential horror questions to discuss. They were all SPIN graduates. She would add a few of her own, a technique she'd learned from Ian as the reporter from hell.

She would meet with her team right after lunch and review the negative questions with them.

There were sure to be some issues come up that George had missed, but her confidence level was high.

After she'd met with her team, she'd call SPIN College to see if Ian could become *Dennis Zonk* for simulated interviews with her team. They could gather in the cyber conference studio to face him.

Tanya again wondered if Ian and Dennis Zonk weren't really one and the same, but she dismissed the idea. It couldn't be, could it?

Chapter 19

Of Course There's A Third Student.

Issues of:

Safety

Economy

Privacy

Meet Police Captain Louise Abdul, BCPD

Louise was a household face in Big City. She had received world attention in 2010 for a daring incident captured on live television.

Through a fluke of scheduling and illness, Louise had one day found herself as acting commander of the Big City downtown police division. It was Hell's Kitchen, with high crime, drug dealing and police corruption, not to mention labour unrest stirred up by their bully union. When the union bosses learned that Louise was suddenly in charge for that day, they decided to stage an illegal protest about overtime and other work issues.

The protest took place at Division DT Headquarters at high noon. TV was there to record it all.

As the black-suited union goons walked across the square, Louise came out to meet them. Cameras and microphones captured every spoken word.

As the 6'7" union leader Chuck Bombastic approached the 5'3" Louise, she stared intently into his eyes. She ignored the other union goons who trailed him. It was a scene designed for maximum intimidation.

Then he made his mistake. "Step aside little lady, we don't want no employment-equity, hiring quota bitch gettin' in our way. Step aside or I'll squash you like a bug and ruin your fancy hairdo."

That was when it happened.

Few saw it coming.

The resulting photograph would become part of the News Hall of Fame and the union's *wall of shame*.

The huge police union boss suddenly found himself staring down the barrel of Louise's very large sidearm. She cocked the gun, placed it right between his eyes and said…

"Under section 24, sub-section 12, paragraph 2 of the Law Enforcement Act, I'm placing you under arrest for threatening a police officer in the conduct of *her* duties."

She smiled when she emphasized the word her.

That was when the giant union boss's bladder let loose. Louise found herself talking to a huge man standing in a puddle, surrounded by live cameras and police officers.

Not only that, but within seconds, every other police officer present had drawn a firearm. Some firearms were very big and fully loaded. But all of them were aimed at the bewildered union boss.

The event became a watershed moment in the end of bully unionism. Unions had become dangerous and intimidating organizations as led and mastered by goons like Bombastic.

The majority of police officers received major pay increases as a result of self-employment contracts. Louise's actions were seen as a turning point in law enforcement and organized labour.

Teachers, nurses and other unionized workers quickly moved to self-employed status, and then worked cooperatively with the employers and organizations they'd fought for years.

Louise became an instant media sensation. She had very little to say, much of it amounted to "*Just doing my job.*" But the coverage was at saturation levels.

Her 15 minutes of fame lasted less than 24 hours.

Then the union boss filed a lawsuit. Louise was under a court order not to speak about the incident. On the instructions of her lawyer, she spent two years saying "No comment" whenever a reporter spoke to her. She would soon be speaking publicly again.

She went to SPIN College, and quickly caught on to the basic principals that ran through all of the training.

She learned about control and relationships in a communications encounter.

She saw the dangers and opportunities of negative messaging.

Threes.

"Control, negative messaging, threes," she would think to herself. It would become her personal mantra and reminder. *"Control, negative messaging, threes."*

The lawsuit brought against her was finally ruled as frivolous and she was awarded damages of over a million dollars. She could speak publicly again.

Louise got a new assignment. She had not asked for it. She thought it might be a set-up to have her fired. It was a new task that was top-secret so far.

She was convinced that what was crazy about the job was that it had very little to do with the work of her police department and more to do with the political aspirations of Police Chief Big Ego.

Louise's new job was to convince motorists to install mandatory electronic transponder chips on all their vehicles as part of a plan to replace old-fashioned licence plates.

When she'd first heard of the task, she had said, "Soon you'll have a chip in my butt, just like we do to our dogs". The Chief had only smiled in that crude way of his. Louise was afraid of this man and this project, but her mother hadn't raised a fool.

SPIN College made it simple. *"Control, negative messaging, threes."*

Louise knew that there was some hidden magic in the combination of message management, issues management and reputation management.

Three basic approaches to communication.

Three simple reminders that enabled her to define the message, develop the content of the message and deliver the message in a wide range of formats.

Control, negative messaging, threes.

All of her SPIN College training was specifically tailored to her potential issues in simple templates.

As Tom Lee had learned about transit planning issues, Louise was trained to deal with the issue of mandatory vehicle chips.

Her critics would have a field day with the issue of privacy, and Louise needed to be prepared.

So it was that Louise started her work at SPIN College. Her first introduction started by finding the threes in her project.

What would be the three most important issues to be dealt with in discussing mandatory vehicle transponder chips?

She remembered how Dennis Zonk had kicked off her very first practise interview.

Zonk Question: "So, you some mouthpiece for the Chief? I hear he's in real trouble on his budget. What the heck are we doing talking about computer chips now?"

Louise had started by saying, "I'm not here to talk about the Chief. No comment."

And the interview had gone downhill from there. Then she read, with horror, the fictional *Dennis Zonk* column that had resulted from her first encounter.

Like Tom Lee and hundreds of students before her, she could hardly believe what Zonk had done.

Like Tom, she had a lot of learning to do and she took it on with zeal.

Within three days, Louise would answer a similar type of ambush question with her Power Pillar:

▶ *Vehicle licenses will be replaced by transponder chips next year. We want to hear from the public about some important issues like:*
▷ *improved vehicle and personal safety,*
▷ *economic benefits, and most importantly*
▷ *the protection of personal privacy.*

▶ *Let's all chip in.*

She had sparklers, too:

Already some insurance companies offer 30% discounts to vehicles with chips. That could be an average savings of over $1,800 on your insurance bill if you live in Big City West and decide to get chipped.

Some drive-through restaurants are offering discounts of as much as 50% off tofu chips and fish and chips for anyone whose vehicle is chipped.

In Big Cities like the former Los Angeles, there was a lot of concern about getting chipped. People learned quickly though. New chip technology had already been developed to protect privacy. The data was stored by private companies whose managers faced strict criminal penalties for any leaks or unauthorized release.

Like the many students before her, Louise learned that messaging needed to be developed, defined and delivered well.

She learned to develop messages that proved she was aware of issues, cared about those issues and was doing her share to deal with those issues. She learned to define her messages in the public interest, using common sense or inarguable language — centred on plain talk. She realized it made her look and sound professional.

She learned to format her messages according to the needs of the encounter, using pillars, supports and sparklers.

Within hours of starting her training, Louise was bridging, baiting and going directly to message.

Within a few weeks, Louise would be facing real reporters. She would never, ever again say "No comment."

Within a few months, Louise would be appointed Deputy Chief of the Big City Police Department.

Within a year, she became the first woman to serve as Big City Police Chief.

As she started to conduct media interviews, she noticed how reporters behaved when she used her SPIN College techniques. At one stage a reporter had asked her directly, "Have you had training at SPIN College? Have you become one of their spin doctors?"

When it happened, she paused slightly, smiled, took a deep breath and went directly to her message. "This is really about finding new ways to communicate."

In her heart, Louise realized there was nothing really new about the way she had learned to use her skills. Spin had been around for years. It was just that some folks kept denying it, and as long as they denied it, nobody believed them. They needed to learn to play **The Spin Doctor's Game**.

Appendix

Playing the Spin Doctor's Game: It's your turn.

Start by developing a core message based on a simple system, like the one from our introduction exercise. Then:

▷ Create a trap question containing a negative word from the list on the next few pages.

▷ Re-define the issue in your own words. Express your main concern, action or vision.

▷ Write three fact-filled statements that *show you're aware*.

▷ Next, three statements that *demonstrate you care*.

▷ Finally, three statements that show you're *doing your share*.

▷ Close with a cliché or slogan.

Feel free to reproduce this page for your personal use.

**Now, go find the ponies.
Good luck.**

**Ian Taylor and George Olds
www.neversaynocomment.com**

Opportunity words from the Reporter From Hell.

Abandon, abdicate, abuse, acrimonious, ageist, agitator, allegations, angry, anti-something, appalling, assassinate

Baby-killer, back-stabber, benevolent dictator, bible baseball, bible-thumping, bigot, blame, blunder, blur, bomb, boondoggle, botch, breeder, bulldoze, bum-boy, bungle, bureaucrat

Carpet-bagger, card-carrying, character assassin, charlatan, cheat, circle the wagons, closet-something, coat-tails, collusion, common sense, compulsory, con-artist, condescending, controlling, copy-cat, corporate welfare bums, corrupt, cover-up, crazy, crook *(see Richard Nixon)*

Dangerous, dangling, decay, defensive, destroy, disaster, disturb, domineering, drag feet, dreadful, drop the ball, drunk with power

Eco-terrorist, eccentric, egotistic, elitist, embarrassed, enough *(as in doing enough?),* environmental disaster, enviro-nazi, evil-doer, *(see George W. Bush)* expert — so-called, exploit

Family values — without valuing families, fast and loose, feminazi, feminist, fiddle while city burns, flak, flim-flam, flip-flop, frantic, fudge the numbers, fundamentalist

Goodie-two-shoes, something-gate, go round in circles, grey-haired, gloss over, gross stupidity,

Hand-out, hard-luck, hard-up, hero-worship, heterosexist, hidden agenda, hide behind *(as in badge),* hide from *(as in facts),* high flyer, hocus-pocus, homophobic

Idiotic, ignore needs of, ill-advised, illegal, illegitimate, illogical, Imelda Marcos, in bed with…, incestuous, incompetent, incomprehensive, incongruous, incriminating, indecisive, insensitive, insubordinate, insufficient, irresponsible

Job-creating exercise *(see bureaucrats),* juggling, jumping to conclusions

Know-it-all, kow-tow *(see racist)*

Lackadaisical, lackey, lacklustre, languish, lemon, let-down, lie, lifestyle, lookist, loose lips, loose with facts, lord it over, lose face or lose control, lost hope, lost cause

Made-up, martyr, mealy-mouthed, mean-spirited, mega-something, mess, militant, misdirected, miserable, mish-mash, misguided, mislead, mismanage, monopolistic, morale, moron, mumbo-jumbo

Nay-sayer, nazi, nepotism, nightmare, not

Obfuscate, old, oligarchy, oppose, outlandish, out of bounds, out of date, out of ideas, out of touch, over-compensate, overdue, overlooked, overpaid, over-simplistic, over the top, overused

Pander, pass the buck *(see bureaucrat),* patronizing, pencil-pusher, pejorative, perverted, philistine, pinko *(as in bed-wetting socialists),* political, Pollyanna, pompous, prank, prey upon, pro-abortion, pro-crime, pro-something, promise

Queer, quitter

Racist, radical religious right *(is neither),* rarefied, red flag, repugnant, revolt, rhetoric, rift, road-block

Sad, sarcastic, screw-up, secretive, selective memory or statistics, self-appointed, selfish, self-serving, senile, sensationalize, separatist, serial-murderer, serpentine, sexist, shameful, slash, slick, silent killer or majority, simmering, simplistic, smirk, snivelling, special interest, so-called, socialist, split, steal, stereotype, strike out, storm trooper, stumbling block, stupid, sugar-coated, sympathizer

Tardy, tart-up, tax dodge, tear a strip off, terrible, thief, time-consuming, those people, torn down, tragedy, traitor, treacherous, treason, trivialize, turn back on, turn-coat

Ugly, undermined, unable, unbelievable, underground, uninformed, unpredictable, unparliamentary, unprepared, unrepentant, untrustworthy, unworthy

Vote buying *(see George W. Bush)*

Wander in the wilderness, waste, weasel out of, weird, white elephant, wildly optimistic, winging it, witch doctor, wormed

Xenophobic

You people

Zealot, Zonk

Readers:

**Do you have an opportunity word
you'd like added to this list for our next edition?**

**E-mail your word(s) to:
spindoc@neversaynocomment.com
or
golds@go4results.com**

Who knows? You may win a prize!

Hope you enjoyed our book, and that you learned some things so you'll Never Say "No Comment".

We've thrown in a couple of extra copies of the **One Minute Power Message** template to help you.

The One Minute Power Message Template

"Our guest speaker today at _____ is _____.

(Name of audience)   (Your name)

_____ works at (with, for, *etc.*) _____

(Your first name)

_____

(**Who** you are)

He/she recently _____

_____

(Something unique about you)

_____ 's job is to (make, do, work with, help, improve, *etc.*) _____

(Your first name)

_____

_____

(**What** you do, with 3 statistics)

The _____

(Issue or topic of your speech or message)

is important to _____ because _____

(Your first name)

_____

_____

_____

(**Why** you do what you do)

When it comes to the issue of _____ , _____

(Your first name)

believes in the old saying, _____

_____

Please join me in welcoming _____."

(Your name)

Please feel free to photocopy this page or share it with co-workers,
bosses, employees, friends.
We only ask that you make **quality** copies
and keep our company name on it.

www.neversaynocomment.com

The One Minute Power Message Template

"Our guest speaker today at _____ is _____ .
(Name of audience)   *(Your name)*

_____ works at (with, for, *etc.*) _____
(Your first name)

_____ .
*(**Who** you are)*

He/she recently _____

_____ .
(Something unique about you)

_____ 's job is to *(make, do, work with, help, improve, etc.)* _____
(Your first name)

_____

_____ .
*(**What** you do, with 3 statistics)*

The _____
(Issue or topic of your speech or message)

is important to _____ because _____
(Your first name)

_____

_____

_____ .
*(**Why** you do what you do)*

When it comes to the issue of _____ , _____
(Your first name)

believes in the old saying, _____

_____ .

Please join me in welcoming _____ ."
(Your name)

Please feel free to photocopy this page or share it with co-workers,
bosses, employees, friends.
We only ask that you make **quality** copies
and keep our company name on it.

www.neversaynocomment.com

Biography: George Olds

George Olds is the President of **GO4RESULTS!**, a Toronto specialty training company, which was recently designated a Provider of Quality Education by the ACTA/CITC's (Association of Canadian Travel Agents/Canadian Institute of Travel Counsellors') ACCESS program.

George is a trainer, writer and speaker. As a Certified Instructional Designer, he is responsible for a range of new seminars that equip students with the skills to succeed based on simple techniques that are easy to learn and remember.

He is a member of the Toronto Chapter of the Canadian Association of Professional Speakers and a proud Toastmaster.

He has 27 years of experience in the travel and tourism business, and has been training since 1990 for some of Canada's largest travel management companies. He estimates he has trained a third of Canada's travel agents.

His course — **Customer Service: It Ain't Rocket Surgery** — shares its title with his upcoming book.

Other seminars George offers include:

▷ **Stepping Inside Your Comfort Zone** (public speaking coaching)

▷ **Polished Presentation Skills**

▷ **Change, Time and Stress Management**

▷ **Dear Editor: Influencing Public Opinion**

And, of course,

▷ **Managing Your Message** (in association with Never Say "No Comment" Inc.)

Attention Meeting Planners and Conference Organizers:

George is an award-winning speaker. His motivational topics include:

▷ **"To Speak Or Not To Speak: Communication And Your Reputation"**

▷ **"Those That Can…"**

▷ **"Customer Service: It Ain't Rocket Surgery"**

▷ **"The Middle-aged Man And The Sea"**

▷ **"Freedom's Just Another Word"**

▷ **"What Do You Do With A Wet Baby?"**

▷ **"I Never Said You Lied"**

For more details,

please check out his website:

www.go4results.com

Biography: Ian Taylor

Ian Taylor spent the first half of his career overcoming a bureaucratic culture that seemed intent on reducing and restricting public communication.

He's spent the second half of his career training and advising his students to talk like real people, communicate openly and present themselves as professionals.

As a former government media spokesperson, Ian's handled front-page issues like aviation disasters, environmental issues, emergencies, strikes, community relations and the day-to-day situations at Toronto's Lester B. Pearson International Airport.

He served as a customer service communications consultant to the Port Authority of New York and New Jersey on their international airports' *World Class Customer Service Project,* until the events of Sept. 11, 2001 ended the project.

Ian has lectured at the International Aviation Management Training Institute in Montreal, where his classes were among the highest rated among students from over 100 countries. One Ethiopian aviation official told him they had no media problems in his country — if reporters got out of line, they shot them.

Ian's a classroom instructor, seasoned communications consultant and an engaging and controversial public speaker. He's a member of the Canadian Association of Professional Speakers and the International Federation for Professional Speakers.

He can custom-design a speech, seminar or presentation for any sized audience and equip them with skills they can use immediately.

His speeches are packed with tips and wry observations of the zany world of public and media relations; as well, he'll create humorous audience interaction. Be careful when he looks for volunteers.

Ian is semi-retired and accepts a small number of training, speaking and consulting engagements annually. He lives in Toronto and Turkey Point, Ontario, Canada.

Attention Meeting Planners and Conference Organizers:

Need a speaker who's contemporary, topical and skills-focused?

Looking for someone whose message will last long after the conference has ended?

Want someone who will challenge your organization to look at issues, messages and reputations?

Ian Taylor's been speaking publicly and conducting training seminars for over 25 years. As the former public affairs manager at Toronto's Pearson International Airport, his "airport stories" are legendary, provocative and sometimes even funny.

The Toronto Star's Antonia Zerbisias wrote about Ian Taylor:

"In an age when cameras are everywhere, when radio is all talk, and TV is all news, media training has become almost essential to career survival. Taylor makes it sound easy. He believes you should always answer the question. The trick is in knowing how to answer it." —May 27, 1996

Some of Ian's current speeches — modified for all occasions:

▶ **Never Say "NO COMMENT:"** Playing the Spin Doctor's Game

▶ **The Message is the Message** — Stop the PRSpeak and the BureaucratSpeak

▶ **Communicating in a Crisis** — The First Two Hours of Messaging

▶ **A Spin Doctor's Lessons for Life** — Everything you need to know about taking control of your life through the eyes of a professional spin doctor who's been there. You'll laugh, you'll cry, you'll hope you never have to see him again.

Never Say "NO COMMENT" Incorporated

Consultants in Issues, Message and Reputation Management

Since 1988, we've served a wide range of clients from the public, not-for-profit and corporate world. We're trainers, writers, speakers and consultants.

Three Training Courses:
The "Manage Your Message" Workshops

▶ Manage Your Message: Questions, Answers and Issues

Our foundation, introductory workshop provides the basic skills in defining, developing and delivering messages in a range of formats. The course works best for smaller classes, with lots of individual attention and help with specific issues. The workshop has lots of flexibility to adapt to your needs — for any size audience.

▶ Manage Your Message: Never Say "NO COMMENT"

This follow-up course focuses on the media encounter, with simulated interviews for print, broadcast and other formats, including help for news conferences, news briefings and news availability sessions. Student interviews are recorded for analysis in class and ongoing learning after the students return home. This training is available to groups or for individual one-on-one coaching.

▶ Manage Your Message: Speeches that Sparkle with Sound Bites

Our writing and presentation clinic will have you expanding on the 3-it formula for longer speeches and powerful presentations. The first half of the course is a writing workshop, the second half involves presenting your material for analysis and review.

We're based in Toronto, Canada and available to serve the world. We accept a small number of new clients annually.

Member

INTERNATIONAL
FEDERATION FOR
PROFESSIONAL
SPEAKERS

Member